W2c

A CONRAD CHRONOLOGY

Macmillan Author Chronologies

General Editor: Norman Page, Professor of Modern English
Literature and Head of Department, University of Nottingham

Reginald Berry
A POPE CHRONOLOGY

Edward Bishop
A VIRGINIA WOOLF CHRONOLOGY

Timothy Hands
A GEORGE ELIOT CHRONOLOGY

Owen Knowles
A CONRAD CHRONOLOGY

Harold Orel
A KIPLING CHRONOLOGY

Norman Page
A BYRON CHRONOLOGY
A DICKENS CHRONOLOGY
A DR JOHNSON CHRONOLOGY

F. B. Pinion
A WORDSWORTH CHRONOLOGY
A TENNYSON CHRONOLOGY

R. C. Terry
A TROLLOPE CHRONOLOGY

Further titles in preparation

Series Standing Order

If you would like to receive future titles in this series as they
are published, you can make use of our standing order
facility. To place a standing order please contact your
bookseller or, in case of difficulty, write to us at the address
below with your name and address and the name of the
series. Please state with which title you wish to begin your
standing order. (If you live outside the UK we may not have
the rights for your area, in which case we will forward your
order to the publisher concerned.)

Standing Order Service, Macmillan Distribution Ltd,
Houndmills, Basingstoke, Hampshire, RG21 2XS, England.

A Conrad Chronology

OWEN KNOWLES
Senior Lecturer in English
University of Hull

MACMILLAN

First published 1989

Published by
THE MACMILLAN PRESS LTD
Houndmills, Basingstoke, Hampshire RG21 2XS
and London
Companies and representatives
throughout the world

Printed in Great Britain by Camelot Press, Southampton

British Library Cataloguing in Publication Data
Knowles, Owen
A Conrad Chronology. — (Macmillan author chronology)
1. Fiction in English. Conrad, Joseph, 1857–1924.
Biographies
I. Title
823'.912
ISBN 0–333–45913–X

To Christine

Contents

List of Maps

General Editor's Preface

Most biographies are ill adapted to serve as works of reference – not surprisingly so, since the biographer is likely to regard his function as the devising of a continuous and readable narrative, with excursions into interpretation and speculation, rather than a bald recital of facts. There are times, however, when anyone reading for business or pleasure needs to check a point quickly or to obtain a rapid overview of part of an author's life or career; and at such moments turning over the pages of a biography can be a time-consuming and frustrating occupation. The present series of volumes aims at providing a means whereby the chronological facts of an author's life and career, rather than needing to be prised out of the narrative in which they are (if they appear at all) securely embedded, can be seen at a glance. Moreover, whereas biographies are often, and quite understandably, vague over matters of fact (since it makes for tediousness to be forever enumerating details of dates and places), a chronology can be precise whenever it is possible to be precise.

Thanks to the survival, sometimes in very large quantities, of letters, diaries, notebooks and other documents, as well as to thoroughly researched biographies and bibliographies, this material now exists in abundance for many major authors. In the case of, for example, Dickens, we can often ascertain what he was doing in each month and week, and almost on each day, of his prodigiously active working life; and the student of, say, *David Copperfield* is likely to find it fascinating as well as useful to know just when Dickens was at work on each part of that novel, what other literary enterprises he was engaged in at the same time, whom he was meeting, what places he was visiting, and what were the relevant circumstances of his personal and professional life. Such a chronology is not, of course, a substitute for a biography; but its arrangement, in combination with its index, makes it a much more convenient tool for this kind of purpose; and it may be acceptable as a form of 'alternative' biography, with its own distinctive advantages as well as its obvious limitations.

Since information relating to an author's early years is usually scanty and chronologically imprecise, the opening section of

some volumes in this series groups together the years of childhood
and adolescence. Thereafter each year, and usually each month,
is dealt with separately. Information not readily assignable to a
specific month or day is given as a general note under the relevant
year or month. The first entry for each month carries an indication
of the day of the week, so that when necessary this can be readily
calculated for other dates. Each volume also contains a bibliography of the principal sources of information. In the chronology
itself, the sources of many of the more specific items, including
quotations, are identified, in order that the reader who wishes to
do so may consult the original contexts.

NORMAN PAGE

Introduction

The varied materials that help us to understand the life and works of Joseph Conrad are slowly but surely being made available to interested students. Yet since Conrad's death in 1924 these published materials have become dauntingly large in quantity (embracing as they do official documents, letters, diaries, reminiscences, bibliographies, and so on). They can also be as far-flung as the author's life itself, which included three countries of residence and touched upon all five continents: 'citizen of the world', a descriptive epithet from Conrad's *Victory*, also has personal application to a man and writer with so many contacts in so many countries and whose letters are now housed in places as far apart as London and Honolulu. As a work of distillation and assimilation, this chronology is designed to provide a clear and compact digest of Conrad's fascinating life as it develops from year to year. Its form – that of a series of diary or chronicle entries – clearly differs from the continuous prose demanded in conventional biography and so caters for the reader who may wish to check a single fact or find an answer to questions of 'where, when, and with whom?' In addition, the main contents are supplemented by a 'Who's Who' and indexes which provide easy access to a wider range of information. Daringly unchronological though Conrad may be in his fiction, the heat and stress of his own unfolding present as a writer can emerge with striking force in the chronological diary-form: its linear sequences seem especially suitable for following the eccentric 'runaway' quality of Conradian composition, the interacting and cumulative stresses during his hectic major period, and the survival tactics he developed to live with serial deadlines and financial neediness. At the same time, this chronology is not situated exclusively in a continuous present. Process and pattern are just as important in rendering a life-history as are grain and texture, and I have sometimes taken the opportunity to stand back and provide larger narrative and contextual direction as a way of underlining significant phases, landmarks and rituals in his career. Some of these directions are made explicit in my treatment of Conrad's major phase as a writer (1898–1914), while elsewhere they remain implicit in the organisation of entries; but, in either case, they should become fully evident to the reader who wishes to enjoy this chronology as a continuous narrative.

Two main emphases are at work in the choice and disposition of material. While attempting to cover the whole of Conrad's life, I have given special attention to the literary career that begins with the acceptance of *Almayer's Folly* in 1894. Hence the first thirty-six years of his life – divided almost equally between Poland and a widely travelled career at sea – are covered summarily in order to achieve a closer day-by-day focus upon the writer living and working within an English context. In the treatment of that literary life an additional emphasis falls on the compositional and publishing history of Conrad's writings, both fictional and non-fictional. The lesser item in the Conrad canon generally receives a single entry which combines date of completion, first newspaper or magazine appearance, and a reference in square brackets to the volume in which it was later collected. Novels and important short stories are naturally treated with greater detail in an attempt to follow their difficult, and sometimes painfully slow, gestation and evolution. In Conrad's case the unfolding drama of composition has many varied sub-plots: it involves the growth into full-length novels of what were originally conceived as short stories; long-term checks and delays with some novels (such as *The Rescue* and *Chance*); and crisis conditions produced by his choosing to work on competing projects at the same time – and this is not to mention manuscripts burnt by fire and sunk with the *Titanic*!

In the treatment of a literary life such as Conrad's there must inevitably be room for considerable flexibility, since the history of his development and reputation can never be divorced from a whole complex of related factors – the history of his illnesses, writer's block, financial difficulties, collaborations, dependencies, his professional reading and the marketing of his fiction. Again, the process by which Conrad unburdened himself creatively often required many others to help him carry the burden – with the result that several of his novels were, in the widest sense, collaborative occasions which brought into play the help and support of friends, fellow writers and publishers. Hence an account of his unfolding career would be unthinkable without detailed reference to a group of intimates and staunch supporters such as Edward Garnett, J. B. Pinker, Cunninghame

Graham, William Rothenstein and John Galsworthy. These and
other figures will appear in the following pages to indicate that
there is more, much more, than a grain of truth in H. G. Wells's
wry suggestion of 1904 that the needy and impractical Conrad
'ought to be administered by trustees' (to Bennett, 29 Mar).

While accuracy of detail has everywhere been sought for in
matters of dating and location, the search itself can easily be
frustrated by notoriously dark places in Conradian biography.
For one thing, parts of his early life still only yield rescued frag-
ments and tentative datings. Even where documentary evidence
is fuller, other indeterminacies and gaps can arise through the
fallible memory, Conrad's self-mythologising, or his self-confessed
proneness to optical delusions about the expanding length and
scale of his work-in-progress. Every effort has been made to
consult and weigh available evidence, but the reader should
be warned that the elusive Conrad, like his own Lord Jim, does
not always emerge in clear and singular outline and that we may
sometimes have to be content with the humanly approximate.
Another obstacle arises from the fact that the Collected Edition of
Conrad's letters, now in the process of being published, has so far
only covered correspondence up to 1908 and will not be complete
for several years. In such a situation Zdzislaw Najder's immacu-
late biography, *Joseph Conrad: A Chronicle* (1983), stands tall among
work in recent decades for its factual accuracy and command of
unpublished material. Boon companion though Najder's study is,
it has still been necessary in preparing this chronology to return
to unpublished collections of correspondence and consult them
afresh – in particular the Conrad–Pinker letters, the main source
for Conrad's work-plans throughout his life. Other refinements
and additions have been made possible through the generosity
of friends and colleagues, who have kindly allowed me to make
use of their work-in-progress.

A special difficulty for the chronologist relates to Conrad's
reading of other authors and works, partly because that reading is
so prodigious as to demand a chronology to itself. But it is also the
case that, while much is known generally about Conrad's revered
writers and about his habit of reading 'professionally' for his own
fiction, one cannot always specify when or how often he read
certain works and writers. Though he read avidly as a seaman,
devoured source-books as a writer, and owned a large library at his
death, he kept no formal diary or commonplace book to indicate

specific times and volumes. In an area where comprehensiveness would be an impossible ideal I have at least tried to indicate the various *kinds* of reading undertaken by Conrad at different stages of his life, though emphasis naturally tends to fall upon those books about which he is most specific – that is, works by friends and contemporaries in manuscript and published form. Some of the general kinds of reading I have in mind can be listed as follows: early contacts with literature and early influences upon the young writer, reading for private professional reasons (of non-fiction as well as fiction), mutual reading of works by writers in the Conrad circle, his familiarity with literature in three languages, books he reread frequently, and the kinds of work he read for relaxation.

As a digest of existing factual knowledge, this chronology owes an obvious debt to an entire community of Conrad scholars, from pioneer figures such as G. Jean-Aubry and J. D. Gordan to more recent scholars such as Zdzislaw Najder, Norman Sherry, Hans van Marle and the editors of letter-collections. Institutions have also played an important part, and I should like to thank the library staffs at Yale University, New York Public Library, the Harry Ransom Humanities Research Centre, Austin (Texas), and the British Library for providing me with direct or indirect access to their Conradiana. On a more personal note I owe a special debt of gratitude to Keith Carabine for generously allowing me to make use of his work-in-progress, and to Hans van Marle and J. H. Stape, who remain good friends despite the task to which they were submitted of reading through the finished typescript: to it they brought many hours of concentrated attention and a fund of rich knowledge.

For permission to use the brief extracts from Conrad's unpublished letters, I am grateful to the following: Henry W. and Albert A. Berg Collection, the New York Public Library, Astor, Lenox and Tilden Foundations; Beinecke Rare Book and Manuscript Library, Yale University; Princeton University Library; the British Library; and the Trustees of the Conrad Estate.

List of Abbreviations

Individuals

Borys	Borys Conrad (son)
CG	R. B. Cunninghame Graham
EG	Edward Garnett
EP	Eric Pinker
FMF	Ford Madox Ford
FWD	Francis Warrington Dawson
JBP	James Brand Pinker
JC	Joseph Conrad
Jessie	Jessie Conrad (wife)
JG	John Galsworthy
John	John Conrad (son)
MP	Marguerite Poradowska
RC	Richard Curle
TB	Tadeusz Bobrowski (uncle)
WR	William Rothenstein

Works

AF	*Almayer's Folly*
AG	*The Arrow of Gold*
Mirror	*The Mirror of the Sea*
NN	*The Nigger of the 'Narcissus'*
OI	*An Outcast of the Islands*
PR	*A Personal Record*
SA	*The Secret Agent*
UWE	*Under Western Eyes*

Collections

LE	*Last Essays*
NLL	*Notes on Life and Letters*
SS	*A Set of Six*

TH	*Tales of Hearsay*
TLS	*'Twixt Land and Sea – Tales*
TOS	*Typhoon, and Other Stories*
TU	*Tales of Unrest*
WT	*Within the Tides – Tales*
YOS	*Youth, A Narrative; and Two Other Stories*

Other abbreviations

CDAUP	*Joseph Conrad: Congo Diary and Other Uncollected Pieces,* ed. Zdzislaw Najder (New York, 1978)
CUFE	*Conrad under Familial Eyes,* ed. Zdzislaw Najder (Cambridge, 1983)
JCC	Jessie Conrad, *Joseph Conrad and his Circle* (London, 1935)
MFJC	Borys Conrad, *My Father: Joseph Conrad* (London, 1970)
Najder	Zdzislaw Najder, *Joseph Conrad: A Chronicle* (Cambridge, 1983)
PMMag	*Pall Mall Magazine*
RAC	Royal Automobile Club

A Note on Names, Titles, Locations and Money

Though the name 'Joseph Conrad' is an anglicised form first adopted in 1894, I have used the abbreviation JC throughout, with a plural form (JCs) to indicate family activities. In line with common critical practice the abbreviation for Ford Madox Hueffer (FMF) derives from the surname (Ford) he adopted in 1919, with a plural form (FMFs) being used for family activities and the Hueffer surname retained only for his wife, from whom Ford was estranged in 1909.

For the sake of clarity and economy, items in the Conrad canon are normally identified by their publication titles as found in Dent's Collected Edition (1946–54). Details of the various titles used by Conrad during composition and, in the case of shorter items, for first magazine publication can be found in Theodore G. Ehrsam's *A Bibliography of Joseph Conrad* (Metuchen, NJ, 1969).

Where the context does not make it clear, all references to streets, business premises, theatres, hotels and cafés are to a London location. All singular verbs which lack an explicitly identified subject in the following chronology refer to Conrad.

Present-day equivalents for sums of money referred to in this chronology can be arrived at by multiplying amounts by approximately 60 (figure supplied by Midland Bank, Statistics Unit, London).

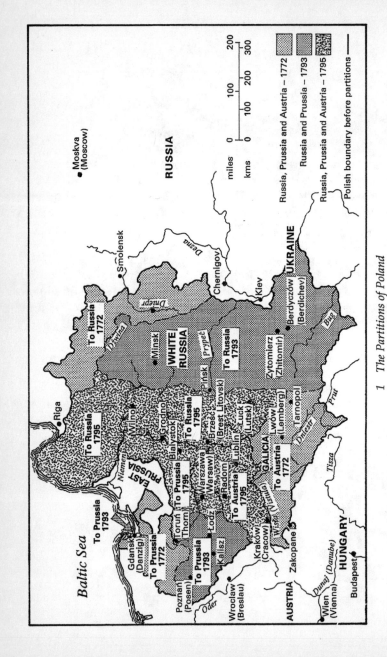

1   *The Partitions of Poland*

(Reproduced from Cedric Watt's *A Preface to Conrad* [Longman, 1982] by kind permission of the author)

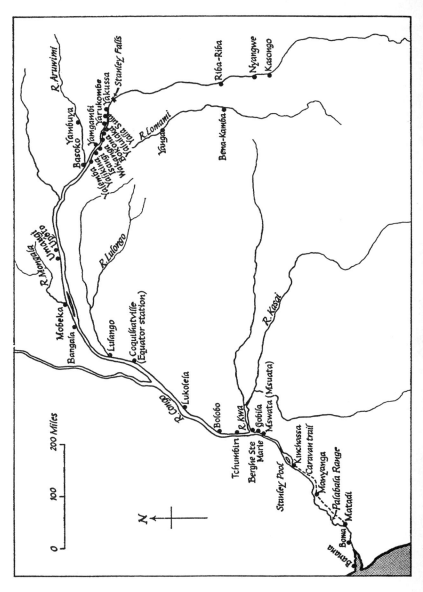

2 *The River Congo*

A Conrad Chronology

Early Years (1857–73)

1857 (3 Dec) Józef Teodor Konrad Nałecz Korzeniowski is born in Berdyczów in the Ukraine, a part of Poland annexed by Russia since 1793. He is the only child of Apollo Korzeniowski, a writer, translator and Polish patriot (born 1820), and Ewa (*née* Bobrowska, born 1832), who were married on 4 May 1856. Both parents are members of the landowning or *szlachta* class, though from families very different in their traditions and commitments. The politically active Korzeniowskis espouse soldierly and chivalric qualities, upholding the tradition of patriotic action against Russia in the name of national independence and democratic reforms. In the view of Tadeusz Bobrowski (TB), chief spokesman for his family, the Bobrowskis traditionally affirm the tenets of enlightened conservatism, trusting to 'realistic' political adjustment and conciliation as the means to eventual Polish autonomy; no less patriotic than Apollo in his view, TB asserts the need 'to make a sober assessment of our position, to abandon our traditional dreams, to draw up a programme of national aims for many years to come, and above all, to work hard, to persevere, and to observe a strict social discipline' (*CUFE*, p. 36). These varied inheritances come together in the three fore-names chosen for JC, the first two derived from his grandfathers and the third (Konrad) from the name of the hero and Romantic patriot in Adam Mickiewicz's dramatic poem *Dziady* (1832). JC is also a Nalecz Korzeniowski, 'Nałecz' being 'the heraldic name of the family coat-of-arms' (Baines, *Joseph Conrad: A Critical Biography*, p. 1).

1859 After Apollo's financial failure as an estate manager in Derebczynka, the family move at the beginning of the year to Żytomierz, where Apollo can devote himself to his literary and political ambitions. He writes and translates extensively, helps to run a publishing company, and is actively engaged in underground patriotic movements.

1

1861 By May, Apollo has moved to Warsaw (scene of recent patriotic demonstrations) ostensibly to establish a new literary journal, *Dwutygódnik*, but mainly to devote himself to clandestine political activity. Ewa writes to Apollo on 20 July that 'Konrad is growing into a lovely boy. He has a heart of gold and with the ground you prepare for him there should be no problems with his conscience and mind. He often goes to church with me . . . .' When she and her son join Apollo in October, their home becomes a centre for the underground Committee of the Movement. On 20 October, Apollo is arrested and spends seven months in the Warsaw Citadel; Ewa too is later accused of unlawful revolutionary activity.

1862 After military trial Apollo and Ewa are sentenced on 9 May to exile and, with their four-year-old son, are escorted under police supervision to Vologda, 300 miles north-east of Moscow. Ewa and her son fall ill before the journey is finished in mid-June – she through physical collapse, he with pneumonia. The harsh Russian conditions, soon to take their toll upon the health of the whole family, are graphically evoked in Apollo's early letter from Vologda to the Zagórskis (Najder, p. 17).

1863 At the new year TB presents JC with the gift of a book, *Les Anges de la terre* (1844) by A.E. de Saintes. Later in the month the Korzeniowskis are allowed to move south to Chernikhov, near Kiev, where news of the 1863 insurrection and its defeat meets them on arrival. Ewa and her son are permitted three months leave in the summer for medical treatment and to visit her relatives at Nowochwastów, the estate of TB's parents-in-law. Already a 'great reader' (*PR*), JC has some of his first lessons in French here. On her return to exile Ewa, now suffering from tuberculosis, begins to deteriorate in health.

1864–5 Apollo completes many of his translations during this period in Chernikhov, and it is here that JC makes a first contact with imaginative literature by way of Dickens' *Nicholas Nickleby* (1839) and Shakespeare's *The Two Gentlemen of Verona* (1594). In early childhood he is also introduced to Polish Romantic poetry through the works of Mickiewicz and Słowacki, which Apollo recites aloud. When Ewa dies (18 Apr 1865), father and son are left in lonely companionship, the now-melancholy Apollo overseeing the education of his 'poor little orphan' as best he can and kept afloat by an allowance from TB. JC later remembers his father during this period as 'A man of great sensibilities; of exalted and dreamy temperament; with a terrible gift of irony and of gloomy disposition; withal of strong religious feeling degenerating after the loss of his wife into mysticism touched with despair' (to EG, 20 Jan 1900).

1866 JC's long summer stay with his maternal grandmother, Teofila Bobrowska, at Nowochwastów is marred by illness in August. Accompanied by her, he returns to Chernikhov for the autumn but still suffers from migraine, nervous fits and epileptic symptoms. His grandmother takes him to Kiev for medical treatment and then back to Nowochwastów; in December he requires further treatment in Kiev, where he remains until the following spring.

1867 In spring, on another visit to the country, JC falls ill with German measles and requires medical treatment in Zytomierz. In the summer, with TB, he has his first sight of the sea in Odessa. Father and son are reunited in autumn, when the boy probably makes a first contact with sea literature through his father's translation of Hugo's *Les Travailleurs de la mer* (1866). By December the now ailing Apollo is granted a permit to leave Chernikhov for Madeira or Algiers.

1868 (Feb) The seriously ill Apollo and his son finally settle in Lwów in Austrian Poland.

(17 Mar) Apollo reports that he intends to bring up JC 'not as a democrat, aristocrat, demagogue, republican, monarchist . . . but only as a Pole' (*CUFE*, p. 112).

(Apr) They spend some time at the Mniszek family estate near Przemyśl, where Apollo first considers a move to Cracow to edit *Kraj*, a periodical soon to be established.

(June) Deteriorating health takes Apollo, with his son, to Topolnica, where he undergoes a four-mouth cure before returning to Lwów later in the year.

(Oct) Apollo is planning a novel 'about the depravity flowing to us from Mosow'; JC – now able to write fluently – is remembered as having produced about this time literary pieces 'on the theme of the insurgents fighting against the Muscovites' (Najder, p. 27).

By the end of the year responsibility for JC's education passes from Apollo to a young tutor.

1869 Apollo and his son move in February to Cracow, where Apollo dies on 23 May. His funeral on the 26th turns into a huge patriotic demonstration, with the 11-year-old JC at the head of a procession of several thousand people. Temporarily placed in a boarding school after the funeral, the orphan is looked after by his father's close friend, Stefan Buszczyński, and also by his devoted grandmother, who takes him to Bavaria for the summer and, on their return to Cracow, looks after her beloved 'Konradek' for the rest of the year.

1870–3 On 2 August 1870 official guardianship of the youth is granted to Teofila Bobrowska and Count Wladyslaw Mniszek, with JC going to live at his grandmother's Cracow flat from late 1870 to May 1873. It is his uncle TB, however, who is most influential in overseeing his education and financial affairs. Little is known of his formal education at this time, though the boy's persistent ill-health (he continues to suffer from severe headaches and nervous attacks) means that it is probably spasmodic and irregular. His informal reading (much of it in French as well as Polish translation) seems to have expanded dramatically, taking in such authors as Marryat, Cooper, Mungo Park, Sir Leopold McClintock, Scott and Thackeray, and works such as Dickens' *Bleak House* (1853), Cervantes' *Don Quixote* (1605–15), Lesage's *Gil Blas* (1715–35), Turgenev's *Smoke* (1867) and *A Nest of Gentlefolk* (1858), and Louis Garneray's *Voyages, aventures et combats* (1853).

An attempt to gain Austrian citizenship for the boy is unsuccessful in 1872. In that same year he surprises his relatives by expressing the desire to go to sea, a romantic ambition no doubt fired by his reading of light sea literature and one apparently viewed by TB as a scandalous 'betrayal of patriotic duties' (*CUFE*, p. 141). His studies are placed in the hands of a private tutor, Adam Marek Pulman, a medical student who accompanies him on regular summer travels. On one of these summer breaks to Switzerland in 1873 Pulman is probably requested to try to dissuade JC, 'an incorrigible, hopeless Don Quixote' (*PR*), from his steadily growing desire to go to sea. On their return in August, TB arranges for the boy to live in Lwów with Antoni Syroczyński, who runs a boarding house for boys orphaned by the 1863 insurrection.

Sea Years (1874–93)

1874 Removed from Lwów in September and with preparations already afoot to further his desire to go to sea, the 16-year-old youth departs for Marseille on 13 October and makes what will later be described in *PR* as 'a, so to speak, standing jump out of his racial surroundings and associations'. One determining reason for his departure is that, as the son of a political prisoner, he is liable to conscription in the Russian army. On the other hand, his status in France as a Russian subject seeking employment in French vessels will be complicated by the recruitment law which lays down that 'tout homme au dessus de quinze ans ne peut cesser d'être sujet russe, à moins d'avoir satisfait complètement aux obligations militaires ou d'en être exempté' (*Annuaire de législation étrangère*, 1875, p. 606). Travelling via Vienna, Zürich and Lyon, he arrives in Marseille to be looked after by Wiktor Chodźko, a Polish seaman living near Toulon. Chodźko's friend Baptistin Solary recommends JC to Jean-Baptiste Delestang, owner of a shipping firm and a Carlist sympathiser. His sea life begins on 15 December when he sails as a passenger on the Delestang-owned *Mont-Blanc*, a barque bound for St Pierre, Martinique.

1875 The *Mont-Blanc* arrives in St Pierre on 6 February and, after a seven-week stay, leaves on 31 March, returning to Marseille on 23 May after a round-passage of five months. Soon he repeats the same voyage in the *Mont-Blanc*, this time as an apprentice, leaving on 25 June for St Pierre, where the ship arrives on 31 July. On 23 September she departs via St Thomas (Virgin Islands) for Cap Haïtien (Haïti), where she remains during October and which she leaves on 1 November. After a total voyage of six months JC arrives on 23 December in Le Havre, from where he returns to Marseille via Paris.

1876 The first six months of the year find JC enjoying the social, cultural and bohemian excitements of Marseille – where 'the puppy opened his eyes', as he later comments (to JG, 8 May

1905). Its bustling café and harbour life is an obvious attraction and no doubt accounts for the young man's substantial overspending. JC also enjoys the thriving theatre and opera (Sardou, Scribe, Meyerbeer, Offenbach and, above all, Bizet's *Carmen*). He appears to neglect the educational study expected of him by TB, who also suspects himself of being tricked into sending extra funds by a financial intrigue devised by JC, Chodźko and Solary.

Shore-life comes to a close on 10 July when JC sails as a steward in the *Saint-Antoine*, a Delestang-chartered barque bound for Martinique. Its crew includes two men who will reappear in JC's memoirs and fiction – the first mate Dominique Cervoni (prototype of Nostromo and Peyrol) and an apprentice, César Cervoni, apparently unrelated. Entries in the ship's Agreement and Account of Crew indicate beyond doubt that on arrival in Martinique on 18 August the *Saint-Antoine* stayed in the St Pierre roads and did *not* visit ports in Colombia and Venezuela. It remains a possibility that JC absented himself from ship temporarily, but visits to South American ports would only be possible in regular mail steamers, not under sail, in order to be back in time to join the ship for her return voyage to France. Five weeks later, on 25 September, the *Saint-Antoine* departs for St Thomas (Virgin Islands), arriving on the 27th for a fortnight's stay. She takes a further fortnight to reach Port-au-Prince, Haïti (26 Oct) and leaves from Mirogoâne on 23 December for Marseille. On 3 December JC is 19.

1877 Arriving back in Marseille on 15 February, JC is prevented by illness from rejoining the *Saint-Antoine* when she sails on 31 March. A disagreement with Delestang in early summer leaves him in the position of having to look for gainful employment. Unsettled and short of money, JC writes to TB about his future prospects, including plans to join the British Merchant Marine (with a view to naturalisation) and even to enlist in the Japanese navy. The later part of the year (until Mar 1878) constitutes one of the most mysterious periods in JC's life, a period which begins when TB sends his nephew 3000 francs in the belief that he is embarking on a world voyage. The main sources for one version of JC's activities during late 1877, his own later highly coloured accounts in *Mirror* and *AG*, suggest that as one of a syndicate of four and in the company of the Cervonis he is engaged in running guns to Spain for the Carlist cause in the *Tremolino*, with the outcome that the ship is deliberately sunk to prevent capture and César Cervoni ignominiously drowned. The smuggling venture is organised by 'Rita de Lastaola', with whom JC supposedly falls in love and on whose behalf he is wounded in a duel in March 1878. Some of this account is patently disqualified by known facts (for example, César Cervoni was alive well beyond 1878) and factual corroboration for many of the events is slight. In addition, the whole episode as later written about by JC must be reassessed in the light of the version given by TB when he arrives in Marseille in March 1878.

1878 A different and more prosaic account by TB suggests that after difficulties concerning JC's status in French boats, financial setbacks over a proposed smuggling expedition and an indiscreet gambling episode in Monte Carlo, he returns to Marseille virtually penniless and attempts suicide by shooting himself in the chest, though without serious injury. In early March TB hears that his nephew is 'wounded', leaves Kiev on 8 March, and arrives on the 11th to find JC out of bed and mobile. He describes him as 'not a bad boy, only one who is extremely sensitive, conceited, reserved, and in addition excitable' (TB to Buszczyński, 24 Mar 1879). In Marseille TB consults with Richard Fecht, a German friend of JC's, and settles his nephew's debts. A career in French ships now closed to JC, it is decided that he will join the British Merchant Marine.

(24 Apr) After payment of a considerable deposit, JC sails as unofficial apprentice in the *Mavis*, a British steamer bound from Marseille for the Sea of Azov via Constantinople. In the *Mavis* he makes his first sustained contact with the English language and the Merchant Marine.

(10 June) He first sets foot on English soil at Lowestoft and travels immediately to London.

(8 July) A letter from TB taxes him for overspending.

(11 July) He sails in the *Skimmer of the Seas* as an ordinary seaman and nicknamed 'Polish Joe' by the crew, making three voyages from Lowestoft to Newcastle and back before he signs off.

After 10 weeks service, during which he learns much English nautical terminology, he signs off the *Skimmer* (23 Sep) and returns to London. Soon after, he joins the wool clipper *Duke of Sutherland* as ordinary seaman, sailing from London (15 Oct) for Australia. On the outward passage he celebrates his twenty-first birthday (3 Dec) and rounds the Cape of Good Hope for the first time.

1879 (31 Jan) The *Duke of Sutherland* arrives in Sydney, with JC remaining on board as watchman during her five-month stay. Here he makes a first contact with Flaubert's fiction through *Salammbô* (1862) and is first attracted to the possibility of working in the Malay Archipelago.

(5 July) The *Duke of Sutherland* leaves Sydney and, after a round-voyage of one year, arrives in London on 19 October. With his uncle's encouragement, JC now plans to take his second mate's examination and obtain British naturalisation, though TB also points out (26 Oct) that 'staying on land has always had an inauspicious influence upon you'.

(11 Dec) Soon after his twenty-second birthday, he enlists as ordinary seaman in the steamship *Europa* and next day leaves London via Penzance for the Mediterranean, with ports of call in Italy and Greece.

1880 The *Europa* arrives back in London on 30 January, JC having had an unpleasant trip and a disagreement with her captain. In London for the next six months, he first lodges at Tollington Park St, near Finsbury Park, and then (May) in the home of William Ward at 6 Dynevor Rd, Stoke Newington (his London base until November 1886), where he comes to know A. P. Krieger, a fellow lodger. About this time he also meets G. F. W. Hope, and the three soon become staunch friends. JC attends a special tutorial course to prepare for his second mate's examination, which he successfully passes on 28 May. Enlisting as third mate in the iron clipper *Loch Etive* – his first berth as an officer – he sails from London on 22 August and arrives in Sydney on 24 November, remaining there until the new year.

1881 (11 Jan) The *Loch Etive* leaves Sydney and, after a total voyage of eight months, arrives in London on 25 April, when JC signs off.

(20 May) He defers a projected meeting with his uncle and is soon in financial difficulty following a failed speculative venture. Expecting his nephew to be soon bound for Australia, TB suggests (28 June) that he might write some articles on life at sea for Polish magazines.

(10 Aug) In a desperate letter to his uncle requesting £10, JC alleges that after sustaining an injury on a recent voyage in the *Annie Frost* he has been in hospital and lost all of his baggage. No documentary evidence exists to support this claimed 'disaster', which is probably an invention – not the first or the last on JC's part – to extract more money from his guardian.

(19 Sep) After signing on as second mate in the *Palestine*, an old barque bound for Bangkok, JC begins an ill-fated voyage whose erratic progress later forms the basis of the narrative in 'Youth' (where the ship is renamed the *Judea*).

(21 Sep) The *Palestine* sails from London, stopping at Gravesend and then taking three weeks to reach Newcastle (20 Oct), where she remains a further five weeks picking up a cargo of coal.

(29 Nov) Leaving for Bangkok, the ship loses a mast and springs a leak in the English Channel.

(24 Dec) With the crew refusing to continue, she puts back for Falmouth.

1882 The *Palestine* remains in Falmouth for the next eight months undergoing repairs, JC deciding to stay with the ship as a way of accumulating service in preparation for his first mate's examination. Like the young narrator in 'Youth', he is likely to have had a small library of books to occupy his days – a complete set of Byron's poems (bought on a trip to London), a one-volume edition of Shakespeare, Carlyle's *Sartor Resartus* (1836) and Frederick Burnaby's *A Ride to Khiva* (1876).

(17 Sep) The *Palestine* leaves Falmouth for Bangkok with a new crew.

1883 (14 Mar) Spontaneous combustion causes a coal-gas explosion in the *Palestine* and forces the crew to abandon ship when she catches fire in Bangka Strait, off Sumatra. The crew take to boats and next day (the *Palestine* now a mass of fire) row the short distance to Muntok on Bangka Island.

(21 Mar) Officers and crew leave for Singapore in the SS *Sissie*, arriving the day after.

(2 Apr) A Marine Court of Enquiry exonerates officers and crew from all blame.

(3 Apr) The crew is discharged. JC, hoping for a homeward berth, stays in Singapore until mid-April. He finally sails home as a passenger and arrives in London at the end of May.

(July) A plan to take his chief mate's examination on the 4th is apparently thwarted by JC's failure to meet Board of Trade requirements for length of service. Later in the month he travels to meet his uncle in Marienbad.

(12 Aug) They go to Teplice for the rest of the month. TB donates a sum of money to cover the cost of British naturalisation and promises £350 to enable JC to invest in Barr, Moering and Co., a firm of shipping agents.

(10 Sep) JC signs on as second mate in the *Riversdale*, a clipper bound from London to the East. She sails three days later and stays over in Port Elizabeth, South Africa, from 7 December until 9 February.

1884 (6 Apr) After a seven-month voyage the *Riversdale* arrives at Madras, where, following a dispute with the captain, JC is relieved of his position and officially discharged on the 17th. He immediately travels overland to Bombay.

(28 Apr) He signs on as second mate in the *Narcissus*, a clipper to be memorialised later in the title of JC's first sea story, *The Nigger of the 'Narcissus'*. During the voyage (which begins on 5 June) Joseph Barron, an able seaman and apparently an American negro, dies at sea.

(16 Oct) After 134 days at sea the *Narcissus* arrives in Dunkirk, JC returning with a small pet monkey among his belongings.

(17 Nov) Having successfully appealed against the bad-conduct record given to him by Captain McDonald of the *Riversdale*, he is allowed by the London Marine Board to sit for his first mate's examination, which he fails at the first attempt (a fact unmentioned in *PR*).

(3 Dec) He successfully repeats the examination on his twenty-seventh birthday, and sets about looking for a job.

1885 After a lengthy search for a new berth, JC signs on as second mate in the *Tilkhurst*, a clipper leaving Hull (27 Apr) for the East but first stopping over in Penarth (13 May) for cargo. During her month-long stay, JC establishes contact in Cardiff with an émigré Pole and his family, the Kliszczewskis. His letters later in the year from the East to Joseph Spiridion Kliszczewski, thanking him for copies of the *Daily Telegraph* and London *Evening Standard*, represent the earliest surviving examples of his written English. In his letter of 13 October he admits, 'When speaking, writing or thinking in English the word Home always means for me the hospitable shores of Great Britain.'

(10 June) The *Tilkhurst* sails for Singapore.

(22 Sep) She arrives in Singapore, remaining there for a month.

(19 Oct) She leaves for Calcutta, arriving on 19 November for a seven-week stay in port.

(Late Nov) JC is determined to pass his master's examination next year, but also restless and dissatisfied with the Merchant Marine and earnestly contemplating an investment in a whaling venture as a way of making 'a fresh start in the world' (to Kliszczewski, 25 Nov).

1886 (12 Jan) The *Tilkhurst* sails from Calcutta.

(16 June) After a total voyage of 14 months, she arrives in Dundee.

(17 June) JC signs off and leaves for London. Letters from TB again urge him to think of obtaining his master's certificate and British naturalisation. However, the early summer finds JC restless, testing his options, and exploring the possibility of a job on shore in partnership with Krieger. Another option possibly presents itself in the form of a literary competition in *Tit-Bits*, which offers 20 guineas for the best article by a seaman on 'My Experiences as a Sailor' (closing date for entries, 31 July) and for which JC may have written a short story, 'The Black Mate', apparently his first exercise in fiction.

(28 July) Not surprisingly perhaps, a first attempt at the master's examination is unsuccessful.

(18 Aug) Happier news arrives when he officially becomes a naturalised British subject (one of his sponsors being Hope when he applies on 2 July).

(10 Nov) Maintaining silence about his first examination failure in letters to TB (as in the later *PR*), JC retakes his master's examination and can say that he is 'now a British master mariner beyond a doubt' (*PR*).

(28 Dec) He signs on as second mate in the *Falconhurst*, leaving London for Penarth.

1887 After a five-day voyage JC signs off on 2 January, no doubt taking the chance to visit the Kliszczewskis in Cardiff. Shortly afterwards, he obtains a position in the temporarily captainless *Highland Forest*, whose loading he supervises in Amsterdam, before signing on as first mate and sailing for Java on 18 February. On the voyage JC sustains a back injury, probably being hit by a falling spar. When the ship arrives in the Samarang roads on 20 June, he is advised by a local doctor to go to Singapore for hospital treatment: accordingly he signs off (1 July), leaving Samarang in the SS *Celestial* the next day and arriving in Singapore on 6 July. There he spends some time in the European Hospital and possibly a period convalescing in the Sailors' Home.

Establishing contact with James Craig, master of the *Vidar*, he joins that ship as first mate and (from 22 Aug) makes four trading trips between Singapore and small Dutch East Indies ports on Borneo and the Celebes. A main port of call, the Malay settlement of Berau on the Berau River (eastern Borneo), later provides the basis for JC's fictional 'Sambir' in his first novels. At the Lingard trading post there he meets Charles William Olmeijer, a Eurasian Dutchman, of whom he later says in *PR*, 'If I had not got to know Almayer pretty well it is almost certain there would never have been a line of mine in print.'

1888 After signing off the *Vidar* on 4 January, JC lodges at the Sailors' Home in Singapore for a fortnight. During this stay he is offered and accepts his one and only permanent command – the *Otago*, an Australian-owned barque whose captain has recently died – and, after receiving notice of command on the 19th, hurriedly joins the ship in Bangkok on the 24th. Events and experiences from the 14-month connection with the *Otago* will provide the basis for such later stories as *The Shadow-Line* and 'A Smile of Fortune'.

The ship's departure for Australia (which marks JC's last contact with the East) is delayed until 9 February and the first stage of the voyage complicated by calms in the Gulf of Siam and widespread illness among the crew. Taking three weeks to reach Singapore, the *Otago* stops over for fresh medical supplies and new crew members. On 2 March she sets sail again and, after meeting heavy gales on the way south, arrives in Sydney on 7 May. A fortnight later the ship makes a round-voyage to Melbourne, returning to Sydney on 11 July. From there the *Otago* sails (7 Aug) to Port Louis, Mauritius, via the potentially hazardous Torres Strait, arriving on 30 September. During a two-month stay JC mixes freely with the island's French community and develops a romantic attraction for Eugénie Renouf, to whom he eventually proposes. Finding out that she is already engaged, the disappointed suitor leaves with the *Otago* two days later (21 Nov) for Melbourne.

1889 From Melbourne (where he arrives on 5 Jan) JC then takes the *Otago* to Minlacowie (South Australia) in February and, after a month there, sails with a cargo of wheat to Port Adelaide, where the *Otago* docks on 26 March. At the end of the month he suddenly resigns his command and without delay sails for Europe in the SS *Nürnberg* on 3 April, landing at Southampton on 14 May. In London JC soon takes rented rooms at 6(?) Bessborough Gardens, Pimlico. On 2 July his release from the status of Russian subject is officially gazetted.

During the next few months – one of his longest shore stays for some years – he casts around for a new command and probably resumes work at Barr, Moering. Many of his leisure hours are occupied with reading, and he seems to have developed a special liking for Twain, particularly for *The Innocents Abroad* (1869) and *Life on the Mississippi* (1883). One autumn morning (perhaps after reading a Trollope novel the night before) he sits down to write a story which slowly evolves over the next five years into *AF* and eventually leads 'not only to a novel but, by unexpected circumstances, to a new way of life' (Gordan, *Joseph Conrad: The Making of a Novelist*, p. 178). On 24 October he takes steps to obtain a visa in preparation for his first visit to Poland since 1874. A long-standing wish to go to Africa promises to materialise in November, when, through the agency of Krieger, JC goes to Brussels to be interviewed by Albert Thys of the Société Anonyme Belge pour le Commerce du Haut-Congo with a view to captaining one of the company's ships in the Congo.

1890 (Jan–May) The early months of this eventful and momentous year for JC are occupied by his first visit to Poland for 16 years, the later months by his traumatic expedition to the Congo and an experience there that subsequently demands expression in 'Heart of Darkness'. On 16 January, prior to his departure for Poland, JC arranges to visit a distant cousin in Brussels, Aleksander Poradowski. On arrival in Brussels on 5 February he finds Poradowski terminally ill (he dies on the 7th) and forms a sympathetic bond with his 'Aunt' Marguerite Poradowska (MP). Aged 42 at the time of their meeting, this handsome and cultivated woman, already a published author with influential connections in Brussels and Paris, will become JC's early *intimée* and mentor; he soon feels a 'deep attachment' for her (to MP, 14 Apr). He has a further interview with Thys and then departs for Poland carrying the existing manuscript of *AF* and a copy of MP's *Yaga* (1888). After a 10-week stay in Poland (where he begins ch. 5 of *AF*), he arrives back in Brussels on or by 29 April to find that, thanks to MP's efforts on his behalf, his three-year appointment to the Congo is confirmed. At the company's offices he is requested to make speedy passage to Africa, there to take command of the *Florida*, whose previous captain has been murdered by tribesmen. He rushes back to London, returns to Brussels on 6 May, signs a contract, and four days later departs from Bordeaux in the SS *Ville de Maceio* for the Congo, again with *AF* in his baggage.

(12 June) Following a route along the West Africa coast, JC disembarks at Boma, seat of government for the Congo.

(13 June) A first entry in JC's 'Congo Diary' [*CDAUP*] indicates that he makes the short journey from Boma to Matadi, where, held up for over a fortnight, he meets and becomes friendly with Roger Casement. Waiting to begin his up-river journey, JC is 'busy packing ivory in casks. Idiotic employment' ('Congo Diary').

(28 June) With Prosper Harou (an agent) and a caravan of over thirty carriers, he leaves Matadi by overland route for Kinshasa on Stanley Pool, a gruelling march of 230 miles.

(4 July) 'Horrid smell' of death encountered in the jungle ('Congo Diary').

(8 July) Arrives in Manyanga and spends a 'comfortable and pleasant halt' until the 25th, when the trek resumes.

(1 Aug) 'Glad to see the end of this stupid tramp', comments JC, under stress and growingly disillusioned.

(2 Aug) Arrives at Kinshasa, the Central Station in 'Heart of Darkness', to find that the *Florida*, his anticipated command, has been wrecked on 18 July. Here he probably quarrels with the company's manager, Camille Delcommune, and already considers breaking his contract and resigning. From Stanley Pool a letter to TB apparently voices 'a deep resentment towards the Belgians for exploiting . . . [him] so mercilessly' (TB to JC, 9 Nov).

(13 Aug) Allowed little rest, JC departs immediately in the *Roi des Belges* for Stanley Falls, serving first as supernumerary and then as temporary master. Delcommune is also on board for the 1000-mile trip, apparently undertaken to aid a disabled company

steamer. Starts second 'Congo Diary', with entries finishing on the 19th.

(1 Sep) *Roi des Belges* arrives at Stanley Falls where JC is ill with dysentery.

(6 Sep) When the captain of the *Roi des Belges* falls sick, JC takes over command for part of her return trip, which begins on or by the 8th. Also taken on board is a sick company agent, Georges Antoine Klein, who dies on the 21st. Klein's surname appears in the manuscript of 'Heart of Darkness', being replaced later by that of 'Kurtz'.

(24 Sep) JC arrives back in Kinshasa, now anticipating that he may join a longer expedition and perhaps still hoping for a command.

(26 Sep) A change in the company's plans send him to Bamou, where he falls seriously ill. Before leaving Kinshasa, a weakened and demoralised JC writes to MP, telling her of his deteriorating relations with Delcommune ('a common ivory-dealer with sordid instincts'), of how 'repellent' everything is, and asking her to help him secure a release from his contract.

(Oct–Dec) Existing evidence allows only shadowy glimpses of JC over the next three months, though the period covers his slow journey, partly by canoe, back to the coast and coincides with a bout of severe illness – Jessie remembers being told 'how nearly he had died from dysentery while being carried to the coast when he left the Congo' (*JCC*, p. 13). From Kinshasa JC writes to TB on 19 October, complaining of recent illness and confiding his intention to return to Europe as soon as possible. On the 23rd he is severely ill in Fumemba and on the 27th heads for Manyanga, where he conceivably tries to convalesce. After a six-week journey to the coast, he reaches Matadi on 4 December and soon after sails from Boma back to Europe.

1891 Still severely ill, JC returns to Europe, arriving in Brussels in late January (where he spends two days with MP) and in London by 1 February. Despite ill-health, he looks for employment and in mid-February goes to Scotland on business. During most of March he is confined in the German Hospital, Dalston, suffering from malaria, rheumatism and neuralgia. His uncle offers funds and advice from afar – and in late July warns JC against the dangers of flirting with MP.

After several months of extreme physical and nervous disorder,

JC departs for convalescence and hydrotherapy in Champel-les-Bains, Switzerland, making an overnight stay in Paris, where MP now lives. He arrives at the Hôtel de la Roseraie in Champel on 21 May and, while there, manages to work on ch. 7 of *AF*. On 14 June he cuts short his stay at Champel and two days later arrives home, having again called on MP.

During the summer he makes two trips in Hope's yawl, the *Nellie*, along the Thames estuary to the East Coast. Some time before September he moves to new lodgings at 17 Gillingham St, near Victoria Station, which he uses as a London base until March 1896. At the end of July illness prevents him from starting a temporary job as manager in the Barr, Moering warehouse. He begins work there on 4 August, possibly also being employed as a translator at this time. An early literary exercise, 'The Prince and the Page: A True Fairy Tale for Grown-up Princesses' (a possible translation from an original French fairy tale) may belong to this period; JC presents the manuscript of the tale to Edward Garnett (EG), probably in the autumn of 1896.

Unable to dispel the feeling that he is 'vegetating' (to MP, 16 Oct), he soon gets the chance to serve as first officer in the *Torrens* (19 Nov), which sails from London to Australia on the 21st. The celebrated *Torrens*, one of the fastest sailing ships of the day, is memorialised years later in 'The *Torrens*: A Personal Tribute' (*LE*).

1892 The *Torrens* arrives in Adelaide on 28 February after four months at sea. During a six-week stay there JC rereads Flaubert's *Madame Bovary* (1857) with 'respectful admiration' (to MP, 6 Apr). On 8 April the *Torrens* leaves for England via Capetown and St Helena, arriving in London after a five-month passage on 2 September. Six weeks later JC, again as first mate, joins the *Torrens* for another Australian voyage, departing from London on 25 October. On the outward journey the still-unfinished manuscript of *AF* has its first reader in W.H. Jacques, a passenger and recent Cambridge graduate, who finds it 'distinctly' worth finishing (*PR*). Zangwill's *The Premier and the Painter* (1888) is probably among the books JC reads during these long and uneventful voyages. On 3 December he is 35.

1893 During the last fortnight of the voyage JC is ill and, soon after the ship's arrival in Adelaide on 30 January, takes a week's sick-leave. On the homeward passage (beginning 23 Mar) JC meets two passengers, E.L. Sanderson and John Galsworthy (JG), who, attracted by JC's fascinating talk and wide reading, are destined to become his lifelong friends: he will soon visit Sanderson's Elstree home and accompany Galsworthy to see *Carmen* at Covent Garden, an opera which JC has already enjoyed 14 times. Meanwhile a total voyage of nine months ends when the *Torrens* arrives in London on 26 July.

In the first half of August JC leaves for the Ukraine to visit his uncle, nearly losing the eight completed chapters of *AF* in Berlin. Fortunately both JC and manuscript arrive safely for a stay lasting until the end of September.

Back in London and out of work, JC can often be found at the London Shipmasters' Society office among the company gathered around Captain Froud, though he complains of 'disheartening indolence' (to MP, 5 Nov). According to one account by JC's future wife Jessie, she and JC first meet in late 1893 (introduced by Hope) and after a year's break begin to see each other again in 1894.

(27 Nov) The restless JC signs on the *Adowa* as second mate, a steamer chartered by the Franco-Canadian Transport Company to carry French emigrants to Canada from Rouen.

(4 Dec) On arrival there from London the *Adowa* remains idle when the company's plans do not materialise. According to *PR*, much of ch. 10 of *AF* is written during this period of enforced idleness; JC also occupies his time reading Daudet's *Jack* (1892) and translations of Tennyson's poems in a Warsaw review.

1894

January
10   (Wed) Before leaving Rouen on this day JC begins reading MP's *Le Mariage du fils Grandsire* (1894).
12   He arrives back in London.
17   He signs off; unknown to him at this stage, this marks the end of his professional sea career, at the age of 36.

February
10   (Sat) TB dies, which makes JC feel 'as if everything has died in me' (to MP, 18 Feb).

15   The Greenwich bomb 'outrage' takes place, later to be used
     in *SA*.
18   JC has been unwell for several days.

March
Despite neuralgia and feelings of idleness, JC works on *AF*. In
mid-March he takes the typescript of the first ten chapters with
him when he visits MP in Brussels.

April
10   (Tues) Makes a final drive on *AF* while staying for the next 10
     days at Elstree with the Sandersons, who provide practical
     help and encouragement. Completes ch. 11 and presses on
     with ch. 12. The Elstree group (which sometimes includes JG)
     is fascinated by JC's picturesque yarns, delivered in markedly
     broken English.
24   'It's finished!' JC exclaims jubilantly of the first draft of *AF*
     (to MP), which he goes on to revise in late April and early
     May.

May
 1   (Tues) Receives the first part of his inheritance about this
     time (roughly £120).
17   After revising *AF* until mid-May, he now reports that the
     manuscript is in the hands of Edmund Gosse. An anticipated
     chance of command comes to nothing.

July
 4   (Wed) *AF*, under the pseudonym of 'Kamudi', is delivered
     to T. Fisher Unwin's office. This is followed by a period of
     illness and enervation which lasts into August.
30   Still ill after 10 days in bed and dispirited by Unwin's
     silence, JC proposes to MP that *AF* should 'appear not
     as a translation but as a collaboration' in France.
31   Gives evidence at a Board of Trade inquiry into the manning
     of British Merchant Ships.

August
 8   (Wed) Lonely and in poor morale, JC again stays at the Hôtel
     de la Roseraie, in Champel, for hydrotherapy.

18 In better health, reports to MP that he has requested Unwin to return his manuscript, has two days ago begun a short story, 'Two Vagabonds' (later to grow into *OI*), and is avidly reading – Maupassant fills him with delight, while Anatole France's *Le Lys rouge* (1894) leaves him cold.

September

6 (Thurs) Leaves Champel. Two days later, in London, writes to Unwin to enquire about *AF*; meanwhile *OI* lies dormant.

October

2 (Tues) Again attempts to obtain a command.
4 Learns that *AF* has been accepted by Unwin.
8 Meets Unwin at his office and agrees to accept £20 plus French rights. The first professional reader of *AF*, W.H. Chesson, is also present. On the same occasion (or soon after at the National Liberal Club) JC meets EG, senior reader at Unwin's, who will become his early mentor and lifelong friend. 'I had never seen before a man so masculinely keen yet so femininely sensitive', recalls EG (*Letters from Conrad*, p. vii); less happily, his retrospective goes on to promulgate the myth, partly fostered later by JC, that *OI* owed its entire existence to EG's pressure at this first meeting to '*write another*' (p. vii).
10 Returns the manuscript of *AF* after reading it over for three days.
29 (or 5 Nov) While negotiating a possible return to sea with a Liverpool firm, JC has also been studying Maupassant's *Pierre et Jean* (1888) and fears that he is 'too much under the influence of Maupassant' (to MP).

November

14 (or 21) (Wed) Reports another long interview with Unwin. A planned trip to Antwerp on business fails to materialise.
?26 (or 3 Dec) Has been 'absolutely bogged down' with *OI* for the last fortnight (to MP).
According to Jessie, she and JC renew contact about this time, when JC turns up unexpectedly and takes Jessie and her mother out to dine, the first of several 'jaunts' (*JCC*, p. 11).

December
3   (Mon) JC's thirty-seventh birthday.
6   (or 13) Agonisingly slow progress on *OI* – 'Six lines in six days' (to MP).
24 Receives first proofs of *AF*.
27 Eight chapters of *OI* completed, the novel is now given its final title.

1895

January
5   (Sat) Sends his first critical essay to EG – a preface to *AF*, probably written a few days earlier but not published until 1920 in the Doubleday Sun-Dial Edition.
16 EG pays a first visit to JC's Gillingham St lodgings; JC has read the former's *An Imaged World: Poems in Prose* (1894). About this time EG introduces him to E.V. Lucas at the Restaurant d'Italie.
?30 (or 6 Feb) 10 chapters of *OI* now completed.

February
22 (Fri) Returns from visiting the Hopes in Stanford, where he has been 'in poor shape'; illness has prevented him from making a trip to Newfoundland (to MP, 23 Feb).
?23 Contemplates sending a copy of *AF* to Daudet. While working on *OI*, reads serial version of MP's *Marylka* (1896).

March
7   (Thurs) A meeting with EG cheers him up.
c.8 Leaves for a stay with MP in Brussels, where he pursues his efforts to get *AF* presented to a French audience.
15 Returns home to find an appreciative letter from EG about *OI*.
c.23 Stays with the Sandersons at Elstree for 10 days, four of them spent ill in bed. Arrives home by 2 April.

April
2   (Wed) Inscribes copies of *AF* for MP and Jessie.
12 Works on ch. 17 of *OI*.

29 Publication of *AF* by Unwin (in America by Macmillan, 3 May; unserialised).
30 Sees Unwin, to whom he mentions the possibility of a Polish translation of *AF*.

May
1 (Wed) Leaves suddenly for Champel, to seek relief from 'attacks of melancholy' (to MP, 30 Apr) and to press on with *OI*. As on his trip the previous year, he stays at the Hôtel de la Roseraie.
Soon feeling better and encouraged by the first reviews of *AF*, JC forms a romantic attachment with a 20-year-old Frenchwoman who is holidaying with her family at the same hotel. He and Émilie Briquel spend much time together during the coming month, taking trips and discussing music and authors (Hugo, Daudet and Loti). On the 20th JC presents Émilie with an inscribed copy of *AF*, which she will proceed to translate into French. So attentive is JC to Émilie that the Briquel family appear to expect a proposal of marriage from a suitor whom they take to be an Englishman. According to Jessie, she receives letters from JC during his Champel stay and a visit from him on his return. JC departs for England on the 30th, travelling via Paris, where he sees MP.

June
4 (Tues) Visits Unwin on his return, dining at his home on the 6th.
11 Last extant letter to MP for five years (until Apr 1900). (Various questions arise about this mysterious gap in JC's letters to MP, a period during which they certainly corresponded. Have the letters been lost or were they suppressed or destroyed by MP? Baines boldly guesses that JC had proposed marriage to MP and been refused, concluding that he may well have turned to Jessie 'on the rebound' – *Joseph Conrad: A Critical Biography*, p. 171.)
19 Again dines at the Unwins.

July
9 (Tues) While staying at the Sandersons, JC receives a letter from Harriet Capes, who becomes a lifelong friend.
14 Now works on ch. 23 of *OI* and wishes to consult EG.

24   Begins a yachting cruise in Hope's *Ildegonde* in the Channel
     and North Sea. Unwin is also invited but declines.

August
 7   (Wed) The cruise ends. According to JC, he makes three
     trips to Paris during the next fortnight on a business venture
     on behalf of Hope's brother-in-law, arriving back on the 21st.
     For his pains, JC receives expenses and 200 shares in a South
     African gold-mining company.
23   Dines with Unwin, who contracts to publish *OI*.
26   Contemplates a return to sea as an owner–captain for two
     or three years.

September
16   (Mon) After a year of writing, *OI* is finished; two days later
     it is deposited with Unwin for EG to see.
27   Meets EG to discuss the latter's criticisms of *OI*.

October–December
One of the shadowiest periods of JC's life now begins (until the
end of Feb 1896). Little is known of his personal affairs in the
months immediately prior to his marriage to Jessie next March,
outside of the account offered in her sketchy and unreliable
memoirs. During October JC revises *OI* and finishes correcting
proofs by the 28th. On the 19th a *Spectator* review of *AF* refers to
JC as 'the Kipling of the Malay Archipelago'. In a letter to Émilie
Briquel on 14 November he writes of a recent visit to Unwin's
office to see a first copy of *OI* and informs her that he is involved
in a lawsuit. On the 28th he dines with EG, asking him to consider
Edward Noble's work for publication. Later in the year he begins
The Sisters (never finished [*CDAUP*]). 1895 ends with JC's last letter
to Émilie Briquel, who by next February will also be engaged to
be married.

1896

According to Jessie (*JCC*, pp. 12–15), JC proposes marriage six
weeks before the late-March ceremony. The proposal takes place
on the steps of the National Gallery and is finalised a few days

later when JC presses for a speedy wedding, urging that 'he hadn't very long to live and that there would be no family'. If Jessie's dating is reliable, this unusual proposal of marriage occurred about 10 February. During that month JC meets more than once with EG, who may have warned him against acting rashly. On the 25th JC meets EG's wife Constance for the first time.

March

4   (Wed) *OI* published by Unwin (by Appleton in America, 15 Aug; unserialised).

7   Reports a recent trip to Scotland (probably to Grangemouth, where he goes with Jessie and Hope to view a wooden barque, the *Windermere*, which he contemplates buying). Najder (p. 194) suggests 18–24 February as likely dates for the visit.

10   Writes to Zagórski that his recent refusal of a command means that the 'literary profession is therefore my sole means of support'.

16   Introduces Jessie to the EGs at the Cearne.

23   Is now virtually ready to abandon *The Sisters* in favour of a new project, *The Rescuer* (later *The Rescue*), an ill-fated work which will cause the first major creative crisis of his writing career until he puts it aside too in early 1899. He intermittently returns to the novel – or plans to do so – for many years, but does not finally finish it until 1919.

24   JC and Jessie, though both of Catholic upbringing, are married at a registry office in Hanover Square, with Hope, Krieger and Jessie's mother as witnesses.

25   After spending the night at Gillingham St, the JCs leave for a six-month visit to Brittany via Southampton and St Malo, staying first at the Hôtel de France in Lannion.

April

6   (Mon) Reads the first of the mixed reviews of *OI*; has written 11 pages of *The Rescue*.

7   The JCs move to a house on Ile-Grande and soon meet local inhabitants.

9   Jessie has been unwell, though she is a 'very good comrade and no bother at all' (to EG), again busying herself as JC's typist.

13 Sends the first chapter of *The Rescue* to EG, who praises it warmly.

22 Requests Unwin to send him a Malay dictionary for his present work.

May

16 (Sat) An anonymous notice of *OI* in the *Saturday Review* laments JC's excesses of style but judges the novel to be 'perhaps the finest piece of fiction that has been published this year, as *Almayer's Folly* was one of the finest . . . published in 1895'.

18 Writes to the anonymous *Saturday* reviewer, who turns out to be H.G. Wells, soon to be a friend and a near-neighbour when JC returns to England.

22 During the first of many impasses with *The Rescue* JC has written 'The Idiots', by this date finished and sent off (*Savoy*, Oct [*TU*]). The works of Rabelais appear to divert him at this time.

25 Privately defends himself against Wells's criticisms: 'I will never disguise it [my style] in boots of Wells's (or anybody else's) making . . . I shall make my own boots or perish' (to Unwin).

June

2 (Tues) Slowed up by fits of depression, a miserable JC struggles to finish part I of *The Rescue*.

10 Part I finished and sent to EG, he probably begins *NN* as a short story, though it is soon laid aside.

12 Recovers from a recent fortnight of illness, perhaps the bout of malarial fever described by Jessie in *JCC*, pp. 26–7.

17 According to Jessie (*JCC*, pp. 27–31) the failure of JC's South African gold investments finally occurs on this day, when a director of the gold-mine is lost at sea in the sinking of the *Drummond Castle*. On 22 July JC informs EG, 'A man I love much [Hope] had been very unfortunate in affairs and I lose pretty well all that remained.'

19 Feeling better after a three-day cruise, JC returns to his unproductive tussle with *The Rescue*.

July

3 (Sat) By this date Minnie Brooke, a friend of the Unwins, has visited, and JC has met Charles Le Goffic, a local writer with whom he exchanges volumes.

10 Asks EG to send the manuscript of *The Rescue* to Hope, who will check its nautical terms.

21 'An Outpost of Progress', written during July, is now finished (*Cosmopolis*, June–July 1897 [*TU*]) and sent to EG.

August

5 (Wed) JC's paralysing frustration with his 'ghastly' novel reaches its first climax when, in a 'little hell' of his own, he complains to EG of 'breaking up mentally'.

9 Has written 'The Lagoon', completed by this date (*Cornhill*, Jan 1897 [*TU*]), as further relief from *The Rescue*. The German publisher Tauchnitz takes up *OI* for inclusion in the *Collection of British Authors* (1896), followed by *TU* (1898) – early evidence of growing interest abroad in JC's work.

14 Now temporarily abandons *The Rescue* and lays it aside for a year.

22 Recent reading includes *By Reef and Palm* (1894) by Louis Becke and *A First Fleet Family* (1896) by Louis Becke and Walter Jeffery.

September

16 (Wed) About this date the JCs return to England and prepare to occupy a semi-detached villa in Victoria Rd, Stanford-le-Hope (Essex), to be near the Hopes. Jessie and her mother spend the rest of the month preparing the house while JC stays at his bachelor Gillingham St lodgings.

October

16 (Fri) Dissatisfied with Unwin's terms for *NN*, JC surveys alternative publishers.

19 Having now returned to *NN*, plans to submit it to Henley for the *New Review*.

27 Sends a copy of *OI* to Henry James.

30 EG arranges for JC to meet representatives from Longman and Heinemann (as well as Lucas) at a business dinner, probably to settle on publication rights for *NN*. There now begins a period when JC, guided by EG, is directly involved in the London literary market-place.

November

1 (Sun) EG has also arranged for him to meet A.P. Watt, the literary agent, though nothing comes of this meeting.

6   On this and the following two Fridays JC is in London trying
     to negotiate a long-term contract with Smith, Elder for *The
     Rescue*, *NN* and other short stories, though terms cannot be
     finally agreed upon. Before his last interview with Reginald
     Smith (on the 20th), JC sounds out Unwin again and then,
     over lunch with EG, confirms his plan to have a sample of
     NN shown to W.E. Henley with a view to serialisation in the
     New Review.

December

3   (Thurs) JC's thirty-ninth birthday.
4   Lunches with EG at the Anglo-American Restaurant, bringing
     a further batch of *NN* to show him.
6   Casement renews contact by letter and probably meets
     JC next spring in London.
7   EG arranges for him to meet S.S. Pawling at the Restaurant
     d'Italie during the coming week and then to stay the night at
     the British Museum with EG's parents. Now assured of having
     'conquered' Henley, JC presses on purposefully with *NN*.
22   The JCs leave to spend Christmas with the Kliszczewskis
     in Cardiff for 10 days. There JC gives his first interview,
     published in the Cardiff *Western Mail* on 1 January 1897.

1897

January

1   (Fri) Returns to intensive work on *NN* on arrival home from
     Cardiff.
7   The death of James Wait in *NN* now behind him, JC
     prepares for his final drive on the story.
17   Finishes *NN* (*New Review*, Aug–Dec), followed by two days
     in bed. Revision of the story continues into February.
19   Reads the manuscript of EG's London sketches (never
     published).
21   Jessie is laid up with neuralgia, the first of many health
     problems to come.
24   JG pays a visit to Stanford.
The first foreign translation of a JC work (*OI*) begins this month
in a Warsaw weekly, *Tygodnik Mód i Powieści*.

February

2   (Tues) Plans to enrol as a member of the London Library.
7   Meditates a new short story, 'Karain', while *The Rescue* 'sleeps yet the sleep like of death' (to EG).
13 Receives a presentation copy of *The Spoils of Poynton* (1897) from James.
18 In London, where he arranges for EG to read JG's apprentice work *From the Four Corners* (1897).
25 JC and James meet for the first time, lunching at the Reform Club.
28 'Karain' manuscript sent to EG.

March

5   (Fri) The JCs attend a function at the EGs.
10 Has begun rewriting 'Karain' as a result of EG's criticisms.
13 The JCs move to Ivy Walls, an Elizabethan farmhouse just outside Stanford-le-Hope (until Oct 1898).
24 Celebrate their first wedding anniversary.
26 JG has visited recently to announce publication of his maiden volume.

April

5   (Mon) Asks Kliszczewski for a £20 loan until June.
14 After much rewriting, 'Karain' is now finished and sent off (*Blackwood's*, Nov [*TU*]). Blackwood's acceptance marks the beginning of an important five-year publishing connection, coinciding with JC's deteriorating relations with Unwin.
JC soon turns to a new short story, 'The Return', whose progress is initially delayed by work on *NN* proof revisions and Jessie's illness. His subsequent difficulties with the new story serve to sour the next five months.

May

2   (Sun) JG visits and stays overnight.
12 Sends proof sheets of *NN* for Sanderson to read, JG having already seen them.
25 Meets Pawling in London to negotiate terms for *The Rescue*.
26 Receives a copy of Pater's *Marius the Epicurean* (1885) from EG.

June

2 (Wed) After nursing Jessie through a recent illness, JC takes up 'The Return' in earnest.

11 Pawling visits to go sailing in Hope's yacht and stays the night. Having read the manuscript of *The Rescue*, he secures book rights for Heinemann. JC plans to read Constance Garnett's translation of Turgenev's *Dream Tales and Prose Poems* (1897).

13 Overnight visit by Wincenty Lutosławski, whose account of JC and 'The Emigration of Talent' in *Kraj* (1899) provokes further controversy in Poland (see Apr 1899).

20 Has just read Somerset Maugham's *Liza of Lambeth* (1897).

22 Queen Victoria's Diamond Jubilee celebrations.

28 By this date JC incurs a substantial debt to Krieger, one that will worry him for several years and eventually sour their friendship.

July

18 (Sun) Promises to send EG (who has recently visited) a copy of Flaubert's *L'Éducation sentimentale* (1870).

19 Jessie is now in the early stages of her first pregnancy.

26 Various ailments hold up progress on 'The Return'.

August

5 (Thurs) JC's first letter to R.B. Cunninghame Graham (CG), who has previously written to praise 'An Outpost of Progress'.

24 Sends the preface to *NN*, perhaps written during a recent impasse with 'The Return', for EG to scrutinise.

28 EG returns the preface with suggestions for cutting. (It is published after the last instalment in the *New Review* but not included in the first book editions.)

September

6 (Mon) Sends part I of *The Rescue* (now given its final title) and a synopsis to *Blackwood's* with a view to serialisation. JC will soon begin another unproductive tussle with the novel.

24 'The Return', now finished (unserialised [*TU*]), completes a volume of stories promised to Unwin.

28 Finishes revising 'Karain' proofs.

October

8 (Fri) Sees Pawling in London to expunge expletives from *NN*.

11 Reacts adversely to E.L. Voynich's *The Gadfly* (1897). The last of the *NN* proofs are out of JC's hands.

14 Arranges with EG for a visit to meet the latter's mother (on the 22nd).

15 Meets Stephen Crane for the first time, of whom the day previously JC has written to EG, 'I *do* admire him. I shan't have to pretend.' Introduced by Pawling, the two men lunch, are immediately attracted to each other, and spend the rest of the day together.

26 Invites EG to lunch in London (on the 28th), telling him that he has 'at last made a start with the *Rescue*'.

November

1 (Mon) In London for two days, consults with Unwin and meets D.S. Meldrum for the first time at the Daniel Lambert Tavern, Ludgate Hill.

9 Inscribes a copy of *AF* for Crane. (JC has already sent him proof sheets of *NN*.)

26 First meeting with CG at the Devonshire Club, where they cement their friendship in 'two languages' (to Sanderson, 26 Dec). JC waxes enthusiastic about Robert Bridges' poetry and Humphrey James's *Paddy's Women* (1897).

28 Crane's first visit to Ivy Walls.

24 Still wrestles unproductively with *The Rescue*. Informs William Blackwood that he has read the first two volumes of Mrs Oliphant's *Annals of a Publishing House: William Blackwood and his Sons* (1897).

30 *NN* published in America by Dodd, Mead under the title of *The Children of the Sea: A Tale of the Forecastle* (by Heinemann in Britain, 2 Dec). Sends a presentation copy to James.

December

1 (Wed) Admires Crane's stories, especially 'The Open Boat' (1897).

3 JC's fortieth birthday.

5 The outstanding debt to Krieger causes a rift in their friendship, with JC being consoled by Hope every evening.

7 JC's recent reading includes Stevenson's *Ballads* (1895) and

Constance Garnett's translation of Turgenev's *The Torrents of Spring and Other Stories* (1897).

8   Arnold Bennett thanks Wells for drawing his attention to JC's works and enthuses about *NN*.

9   Defends his literary aims in a letter to W.L. Courtney, whose recent *Daily Telegraph* review of *NN* has described JC as an 'unflinching realist' who does not hesitate to give his story 'the ugliest conceivable title'.

17 Spends the day in London, but misses EG.

23 While pressing on with *The Rescue*, JC awaits a William Morris volume from EG and replies to an enthusiastic letter from A.T. Quiller-Couch about *NN*. 'Twenty years of life, six months of scribbling and a lot of fist-gnawing and hair-tearing went into that book', he tells him.

1898

January
In a letter to EG (7 Jan), JC begins the new year with qualified optimism, basking in good reviews of *NN* – the work by which he considers himself to have come of age as a writer – and resolving to finish part II of *The Rescue* by early February. This mood soon dissipates as he enters a year dominated by a steadily deepening crisis of confidence and self-belief, and punctuated by innumerable creative stops and starts. At the heart of the crisis is the painfully unrewarding struggle to unshoulder *The Rescue*, which involves writer's block, broken deadlines and much frantic self-recrimination. Other indecisions and conflicts contribute to a sense of impasse: divided commitments to the past (*The Rescue*) and new projects (*Lord Jim* and 'Heart of Darkness'); indecision about the career of writer or seaman; the need for freer artistic rein and the constricting pressures of supporting a family through the production of saleable copy. 1898 may be seen as JC's painful initiation into many of the difficulties which are to dog his career until 1914.

8   (Sat) Wells and Zangwill nominate *NN* as one of the best books of 1897 for a competition in *Academy*.

?12 Crane proposes that he and JC collaborate on a play about the American West ('The Predecessor'), though the proposal does not materialise.

15 Alfred Borys Leo, the JCs' first child, is born.
16 Comments on the manuscript of JG's *Jocelyn* (1898).
19 Death of Karol Zagórski, JC's distant cousin. Finishes 'Alphonse Daudet', begun the previous day (*Outlook*, 9 Apr [*NLL*]), JC's first exercise in occasional literary appreciation.

February
 2 (Wed) Meets Crane in London to fix the date of the JCs' forthcoming visit and presents him with an inscribed copy of *NN*. Sends an article on Kipling for publication in *Outlook* (unpublished and manuscript unknown). Work meanwhile continues on *The Rescue* in an attempt to emerge from 'the slough of despond [of] that muddy romance' (to EG).
10 Has recently seen Pawling, who recommends sending the unfinished *Rescue* to America.
12 Makes notes on the Franco-Prussian War, probably for Crane's benefit.
19 The JCs leave to spend two weeks with the Cranes at Oxted, Surrey.
26 The Cranes arrange a dinner in honour of the JCs, guests including Harold Frederic and possibly Ford Madox Hueffer (later Ford: FMF).
28 JC in London on business.

March
 4 (Fri) The JCs return from Oxted, staying two days with the EGs on the way home to show off the new baby.
 5 McClure of New York has paid £250 for American serial rights to *The Rescue*, so easing JC's financial situation but adding further pressure to finish the work.
13 EG promises to come on the 18th and stay overnight.
19 Although unwell, JC dines with Crane and party at the Savage Club.
21 Despite EG's help, *The Rescue* still produces 'positive agony' (to EG).
25 JC and Crane lunch with Blackwood at the Garrick Club, the latter advancing Crane money which enables him to depart for the Spanish–American War as a correspondent.
26 *TU* published by Scribner's (by Unwin in Britain, 4 Apr, marking the end of JC's present connection with Unwin).
29 Recovering from a recent illness, JC ponders EG's suggested

revisions to part II of *The Rescue* but is too afflicted by 'crises of despair' to act upon them (to EG). CG has paid a recent visit.

April

8 (Fri) CG pays a Good Friday visit.

*c.*10 Crane leaves for Cuba.

13 JC in London, but misses CG.

16 Finishes 'An Observer in Malaya', a review of Clifford's *Studies in Brown Humanity* (1898) (*Outlook*, 23 Apr [NLL]), which soon leads to a meeting between them.

24 The United States declares war on Spain.

May

Unwell and held up by domestic difficulties, JC works 'against the grain' for the first fortnight (to CG, 19 May) but probably not on *The Rescue*, of which 'a ridiculously small quantity' has been written (to EG, 18 May). The end of the month sees surprising news of two new short stories in progress, 'Youth', and another called 'Jim: A Sketch'. 'Youth', almost certainly begun in May, is finished quickly. 'Jim: A Sketch', a twenty-eight page precursor to *Lord Jim*, may also have been written this month, though a starting date earlier in the year is possible (and one as far back as 1896 has been suggested). These and other new projects will serve to intensify JC's feeling of frustration with, and animus towards *The Rescue*.

12 (Thurs) Cannot accept an Unwin invitation because he expects a visit from two old shipmates, apparently Paton and Paramor from his *Adowa* days. 'Is the glorious and philanthropic war affecting the book business in any way?' he asks.

June

3 (Fri) Finishes 'Youth' (*Blackwood's*, Sep [YOS]).

4 'Tales of the Sea' (on Marryat and Cooper) appears in *Outlook* [NLL]. Sends first 18 typescript pages of 'Jim: A Sketch' to Meldrum, anticipating a story of 20,000–25,000 words.

7 Determines to lay the 'Jim' story aside to finish *The Rescue*.

11 Has read *Father Archangel of Scotland, and Other Essays* (1896) by CG and his wife.

17 Robert McClure stays overnight and postpones the deadline for delivery of the *Rescue* manuscript.

23 Meldrum visits for lunch to discuss plans for a volume of sea-stories, the future *YOS*.

By late June JC is involved in part III of *The Rescue*, trying to 'make up for the lost 3 months' and 'living in a hell of . . . [his] own' (to EG, late June?). For the next six months he makes little progress with the novel, increasingly paralysed by approaching deadlines and afflicted by spiralling indecisions and debts.

July

12 (Tues) After a visit from the ever-helpful EG, JC writes to him, 'I am waist deep [in *The Rescue*] and there is no going back'.
15 Visits CG at his London residence.
19 Prompted by CG, JC sees Sir Francis Evans of the Union Line about a possible command.
30 Receives CG's *Aurora la Cujiñi* (1898), already seen in manuscript.

August

3 (Wed) 'I feel suicidal' (to EG). He continues to do so throughout a month that brings to a head his crisis with *The Rescue* and finds him trapped between heated self-abasement and prevarication with his publishers. CG's renewed attempt to find him a command at sea arouses no enthusiasm.
13 Looks forward to meeting EG, to whom he writes, 'I see how ill, mentally, I have been these last four months.'
27 EG pays a further visit, presumably to cheer up an utterly miserable JC. Reads Rimbaud's poetry and Edmond Rostand's *Cyrano de Bergerac* (1897) but with little relish. 'I wish you would come to shoot me', he writes to CG.

September

1 (Thurs) JC goes to stay with EG at the Cearne in Limpsfield (Surrey) for a fortnight 'to do a monstrous heap of work', presumably on *The Rescue* (to Helen Sanderson, 31 Aug). There he meets FMF, probably for the first time. From this meeting originates a plan to collaborate and a subsequent friendship and association extending over the next 10 years; JC will later describe FMF as 'a sort of lifelong habit' (to Wells, 20 Oct 1905). It is probably on this visit that EG hears JC give a synopsis of the future 'Heart of Darkness' and persuades him to sit for his first portrait.

27 Travels to Glasgow to explore possibilities of securing
a command at sea. With Neil Munro, whose *The Lost
Pibroch* (1896) he has just read, he sees the recently invented
Röntgen X-ray machine demonstrated by Dr John McIntyre,
a friend of CG. On the last evening attends a symposium at
the Glasgow Art Club.

29 On his return confirms that he will accept the tenancy
of Pent Farm, Postling (Kent), sub-let to him by FMF.

October
3   (Mon) JG has paid a recent visit.
7   JC makes a first visit to Pent Farm and stays the night,
stopping off in London on the way to see McClure.
11 Looks forward to being a neighbour of Wells, whose Sandgate
home is only five miles away from Pent Farm.
14 Brings together EG and McClure at the Restaurant d'Italie.
17 Sends a letter to *The Times* about the SS *Mohegan* disaster,
which occurred on the 14th (unpublished).
20 Has recently read James's *The Two Magics* (1989) and
especially admires 'The Turn of the Screw'.
26 Move to Pent Farm.
28 After consulting EG and Henley, JC reports to JG that he
has finalised a plan to collaborate with FMF on 'Seraphina'
(*Romance*), probably begun by the latter in 1896. Receives £10
from JG while also trying to raise money to help Cora Crane.
The month closes with the hope that he can liberate himself
from 'the incubus of that horrid novel' (to Mrs Bontine,
16 Oct).

November
12 (Sat) Reads FMF's first novel, *The Shifting of the Fire* (1892),
while making desultory progress on *The Rescue*.
16 Calls on, but fails to see, Wells.
17 Though collaboration will not effectively begin until October
1899, JC invites FMF to Pent Farm to read out parts of *Romance*,
a synopsis of which will be constructed in late 1898 or early
1899.
22 The deadline for serialisation of *The Rescue* in *Illustrated
London News* is by this date put back to April 1899. JC
is flattered by Max Nordau's appreciation of his work.

26 Edwin Pugh stays at Pent Farm, followed by two other
    visitors, who, with JC, entertain themselves with a reading
    of Wells's *The Invisible Man* (1897).

December
 1 (Thurs) Begins reading CG's *Mogreb-el-Acksa* (1898).
 3 JC's forty-first birthday.
 4 Enjoys Crane's 'The Price of a Harness' in *Blackwood's*, despite
    depression over *The Rescue*.
13 Looks forward to sending Blackwood a short story in January
    – either 'Jim: A Sketch' or 'Heart of Darkness', which he will
    soon begin.
18 By this date reaches the beginning of part IV of *The
    Rescue*, already put aside to work on 'Heart of Darkness' –
    'for the sake of the shekels' (to EG). After entertaining JG,
    reports that he has finished reading EG's 'A Christmas Play
    for Children'.
21 The multiplying literary and financial crises of the year
    leave JC feeling unseasonally gloomy: 'I toil on. So did the
    gentleman of the name of Sisyphus . . . This is the manner
    of my news' (to CG).
22 JC and FMF call on Wells to find him not at home.
30 With Borys ill, JC is again troubled and gloomy: 'The year for
    me does not end brightly . . . I can't collect my thoughts to
    any purpose' (to Munro, 30 Dec).

1899

January
 3 (Tues) After a recent visit by the Wellses, JC is now reading
    a French translation of *The Time Machine* (1895) and in
    possession of *Wheels of Chance* (1896).
 6 Pressed by Krieger to repay his debt, JC gratefully receives
    an advance from Blackwood.
 9 Sends off a second batch of 'Heart of Darkness', accom-
    plished 'under difficulties' (to Meldrum).
11 Crane returns to England from Cuba.
12 Receives a copy of Maupassant's *Des Vers* (1880).
14 *Academy* 'crowns' *TU* as one of the most promising books
    of the year, its laudation probably penned by Bennett. Of

the 50 guineas prize, £50 is sent to Krieger, leaving JC with an outstanding debt of £130.

29 Borys's postponed christening takes place in Hythe.

30 In London for two days, sees EG, 'publishers and other horrors' (to CG, 2 Feb).

February

6 (Mon) Finishes 'Heart of Darkness' (*Blackwood's*, Feb-Apr [*YOS*]), followed by a four-month break.

7 Through JC, Wells has granted Aniela Zagórska permission for Polish translations of his work; JC recommends Mary Kingsley's *West African Studies* (1898) to her.

14 A further advance from Blackwood helps JC to assuage Krieger.

21 (or 28) Has recently seen C.K. Shorter of the *Illustrated London News*, who cancels plans for serialising *The Rescue*. The unfinished novel is now put aside for many years.

26 Has read William Beckford's *Vathek* (1784) and a recent translation of Abu Zaid's *The Celebrated Romance of the Stealing of the Mare*.

March

8 (Wed) Invited by CG, JC attends a meeting of the Social Democratic Federation in London but refuses to be on the platform; he is introduced to W.H. Hudson there. During the next six months he makes no further visits to London.

?12 Defends James as a writer who 'feels deeply and vividly every delicate shade' (to JG).

25 The FMFs stay at Pent Farm while about to move into a cottage in Aldington, leaving on the 30th.

26 McClure stays overnight to discuss the fate of *The Rescue*.

April

12 (Wed) Gout and depression have kept JC in bed the previous week.

17 Reads CG's *The Ipané* (1899).

23 In response to Lutoslawski, Eliza Orzeszkowa returns to the question of 'The Emigration of Talent' in *Kraj* and attacks JC's 'desertion' of Poland. (This article is reprinted in *CUFE*; on its possible influence on the substance of *Lord Jim*, see Najder, pp. 254–7.)

May

In the middle of the month JC makes first contact with Hugh
Clifford by letter.

June

3　(Sat) The JCs spend a fortnight with the Cranes at Brede
　　Place, near Winchelsea, while Pent Farm is decorated. The
　　two men go for frequent trips on *La Reine*, a boat they have
　　purchased from Hope.

July

6　(Thurs) 31 manuscript pages of *Lord Jim*, probably written
　　and shown to EG in June, now sent off, JC anticipating a
　　story of 40,000 words to be finished by the end of July. *Lord
　　Jim* will prove to be the first of his many 'runaway' novels –
　　that is, a work originally conceived as a short story which,
　　batch by batch of manuscript, slowly expands, complicates
　　and accretes until it far exceeds its expected scope. With
　　equal regularity he will anticipate completion of the story and
　　assure his publishers that an end is in sight, only to find that
　　it still awaits him. In later life he humorously described this
　　process as chasing after his subject for the length of a novel
　　'without being able to overtake it' (to JG, 22 Feb 1924).

23　Anticipates visits from James and Henley during the first
　　fortnight in August.

28　On his return from a short cruise, receives Clifford's *Since
　　the Beginning* (1898).

31　*Lord Jim* now expanding, JC asks for a further advance of £50.

August

22　(Tues) A first meeting with Clifford has recently taken place
　　at Pent Farm. Now 20,000 words long, *Lord Jim* continues to
　　mushroom.

23　Turns down a first approach by James Brand Pinker (JBP)
　　to be his agent.

27　Jessie's relations stay at Pent Farm for the next fortnight.

September

2　(Sat) After a visit from FMF, a weary JC presses on with *Lord
　　Jim*, expecting to finish at the end of the month (ten months

away from its actual completion). From this date composition of the novel runs parallel with revising and correcting of serial proofs.

?10 Describing himself as 'like a damned paralyzed mud turtle', JC asks Crane to come and cheer him up.

17 Invites Meldrum to stay overnight later in the week.

October

6 (Fri) Collaboration with FMF now begins, when he comes to Pent Farm to read out the first chapters of *The Inheritors* (*Romance* having been set aside for a later stage of their collaboration). FMF will be responsible for most of its writing, with JC playing the part of critical reader and reviser during rare breaks from *Lord Jim*, now beginning as a serial in *Blackwood's*.

8 Meldrum visits and stays overnight.

9 JC offers Clifford a detailed criticism of *In a Corner of Asia* (1899).

11 Outbreak of the Boer War.

12 Thanks JG for £20 loan. A long letter to Sanderson prefigures the dejection and strain which steadily intensify during the next two months and culminate in the minor 'breakdown' of January 1900.

24 Now having reached ch. 9 of *Lord Jim*, JC looks forward to February completion.

27 Reads the present issue of *Blackwood's* – *On Trial* by 'Zack' and, in November, John Buchan's 'The Far Islands'.

November

12 (Sun) Prompted by an impatient letter from his collaborator, JC invites FMF for discussions at Pent Farm, where, according to Jessie, the FMFs remain for a fortnight. However, FMF is back in Aldington by the 24th.

23 McClure expresses interest in acquiring American book and serial rights to *The Inheritors*.

25 Back at work on *Lord Jim*, JC approaches the end of ch. 13.

December

1 (Fri) The JCs learn of the violent death of Hope's son and rush to Stanford for the day.

3 JC's forty-second birthday.

17 Estimating that *Lord Jim* now stands at 40,000 words, he asks for another advance.
18 The Hopes leave after a weekend stay.
19 Has read Kipling's *The Seven Seas* (1896).
21 JG visits, or has recently done so.
25 The JCs spend a quiet Christmas at home while, not far away at Brede Place, the Cranes celebrate the end of the year with a performance of *The Ghost*, an entertainment allegedly written by 10 authors, including James, Wells, George Gissing and JC.

1900

January
3 (Wed) The new year begins where the old finished, with *Lord Jim* – now standing at 17 chapters – expanding with each batch of manuscript sent for *Blackwood's*.
6 Thanks and praises Wells for *The Plattner Story and Others* (1897).
20 EG offers high praise for portions of *Lord Jim* he has been shown.
25 For the next month JC is ill with bronchitis, malaria and gout – 'In reality a breakdown' (to CG, 13 Feb). He does not rise from his sick-bed until 11 February.

February
14 (Wed) The JCs stay for two days with the Wellses in Sandgate, where JC recuperates and ponders 'Jim's end' (to Meldrum).
17 The manuscript of *The Inheritors*, now with Heinemann, is accepted for publication by 26 March. FMF is invited for a talk about its last chapter.
18 JG at Pent Farm, reporting that Sanderson has been ordered to the front in South Africa.
19 JC resumes work on *Lord Jim* after his illness.
27 Invites FMF for the next week.

March
3 (Sat) Has read Constance Garnett's translation of Turgenev's *The Jew* (1899).
26 Has been 'cutting and slashing' whole paragraphs out of *Lord Jim* (to EG).

April

2	(Mon) MP arrives for a week's stay and suggests that the JCs visit Knokke, Belgium, in the summer; she meets the FMFs (at lunch on Wednesday) and also JG.

3	JC sends a batch of *Lord Jim*, assuming that he has now reached its last chapter, apologising for the 'dragging manner of its production', and promising an end on the 12th (to Meldrum). Its composition will drag on for the next three months.

6	FMF joins JC at Pent Farm for a meeting with McClure and Stephen Gwynn to discuss serial rights of *The Inheritors*.

12	Anticipates a new phase of collaboration with FMF on *Romance* and assures Meldrum that he still pursues an end to *Lord Jim*.

May

6	(Sun) Cancels a planned visit to see Crane, now fatally ill with tuberculosis.

10	Gives several readings to MP's *Pour Noémi* (1900) and has discussed it with FMF.

15	On receipt of the latest batch of *Lord Jim* (chs. 28-30 and part of 31), Blackwood decides that the story has so overrun its estimated length that it must be a separate volume; its title will also need to be changed.

16	(or 23) Goes to Dover, where the dying Crane rests before being transferred to Germany; JC sees him for 20 minutes.

 During this month and the next JC makes a final intensive effort to finish *Lord Jim*, composing the last quarter of the novel in two months.

June

5	(Tues) While not unexpected, news from Germany of Crane's death leaves JC distressed and shocked. He acknowledges receipt of Wells's *Love and Mr Lewisham* (1900) and in mid-June anticipates a visit from JG.

July

14	(Sat) Finishes *Lord Jim* at 6 a.m. and, in high spirits, delivers the last of the manuscript to Meldrum in London. From there the JCs travel via Slough to the Hopes in Stanford for the weekend.

20 The JCs depart for Belgium, where the FMFs await them in Bruges. There JC and FMF plan a working holiday on their new joint project, *Romance*. The party soon moves to the Grand Hôtel de la Plage in Knokke-Heist, where JC spends several days revising and correcting the typescript of *Lord Jim*.

August

5 (Sun) By this date the Belgian stay is thrown into disarray when Borys falls ill with severe dysentery and requires constant nursing. Depressed and suffering from mental exhaustion, JC has a gout attack, with the result that hardly any work is done on *Romance*.

11 Writes to JG, 'I had enough of this holiday.'

18 The JCs arrive home; JC and FMF plan to meet regularly to make up for lost time.

September

13 (Thurs) Having recently met JG and EG separately, JC brings them together for the first time in London. EG has been reading JG's work in manuscript.

19 FMF at Pent Farm, 'working at Seraphina [*Romance*]. Bosh! Horrors!' (to JG).

After this visit JC turns to his own work, probably soon beginning 'Typhoon', which occupies the next three months.

October

3 (Wed) Again approached by JBP, JC goes to meet him in London with FMF and begins an association with the literary agent lasting over twenty years.

6 Reads CG's *Thirteen Stories* (1900).

9 *Lord Jim* published by Blackwood (in America by Doubleday, McClure, 31 Oct), virtually coinciding with completion of serial of November.

10 Feels 'ill and hopeless' after three days in bed (to CG), perhaps a bout of publication nerves.

24 Meldrum gives a dinner party at the Garrick Club attended by JC, George Blackwood, Gwynn and others.

On his return home, JC spends a period working with FMF who leaves him 'half dead' and prostrate for two days (to Meldrum, 31 Oct). He is soon cheered by favourable reviews of *Lord Jim* in the *Manchester Guardian* and *Daily Chronicle*.

November

4 (Sun) JG pays a visit to discuss his work.

7 Reads FMF's *The Cinque Ports* (1900).

12 Receives a letter from James 'absolutely enthusiastic' about *Lord Jim* (to Meldrum, 27 Nov). Has read Olive Garnett's *Petersburg Tales* (1900).

20 Wells's presentation copy to JC of *The First Men in the Moon* (1901) dated.

Sends regular batches of 'Typhoon' to JBP during the month.

December

3 (Mon) JC's forty-third birthday.

11 Attends a dinner party given by JG at Kettner's Restaurant (with Pawling, Meldrum, McClure and EG) and stays overnight with JG.

12 While in London, sees his banker and then asks Meldrum whether Blackwood would stand surety for a loan of £250. Asks for a further loan of £50, which he never repays.

19 JG has recently made a pre-Christmas visit. Apropos *Lord Jim*, JC calls himself 'the spoiled child of the critics' (to Blackwood). Over the Christmas period itself JC and FMF probably meet at Winchelsea to work on *Romance*.

1901

January

10 (Thurs) Finishes 'Typhoon' at midnight and delivers it to JBP next day (*PMMag*, Jan–Mar 1902 [*TOS*]).

c.21 Begins 'Falk'.

22 Death of Queen Victoria; Edward VII succeeds.

February

13 (Wed) Receives a copy of TB's memoirs (2 vols, 1900).

March

1 (Fri) Returning from London after seeing McClure, JC is laid low by illness. A feverish chill, gout and toothache prevent him from working.

Illness spreads through the household when Jessie's mother, on a visit, falls seriously ill; then Jessie herself is 'blind with neuralgia' (to Cora Crane, Tues 9 Apr). JC's only literary occupation is to read the manuscript of JG's *A Man of Devon* (1901).

April
Slowly recovering, JC is visited by FMF and makes plans to stay with him for three weeks at the end of the month, though the visit is delayed while JC attempts to finish 'Falk'.

May
10 (Fri) About this date the JCs go to Winchelsea, where FMF now lives. Joint work on *Romance* continues while JC also completes 'Falk' (unserialised [*TOS*]) and, prompted by suggestions from FMF, begins 'Amy Foster'.
23 The JCs return to Pent Farm.

June
1 (Sat) *The Inheritors* published by McClure, Phillips (by Heinemann in Britain, 26 June; unserialised).
7 A first draft of *Romance* now completed, JC and FMF begin a process of revision and rewriting which occupies the next nine months.
16 Finishes 'Amy Foster' (*Illustrated London News*, Dec [*TOS*]).
17 Goes to Winchelsea for further work on *Romance*, returning on the 24th.
30 JG visits to discuss his work.
During June on a visit to Wells, JC meets Gissing and shows him the manuscript of 'Amy Foster'.

July
1 (Mon) Goes to London, delivering parts of the *Romance* manuscript to JBP, who will forward it to Blackwood with a view to serialisation.
16 Interviewed by a *Daily Mail* journalist.
18 JG visits to discuss his play 'The Civilized' (never finished).
23 JC in London for an interview with Pawling. Informs FMF that he will rewrite part III (as newly numbered) of *Romance*.
25 After unsuccessful manoeuvrings with life-insurance policies, FMF lends JC £100, a debt unpaid for many years. Jessie is ill and looked after by her mother.

August

2   (Fri) JC defends *The Inheritors* in a letter to the *New York Times*, published on the 24th.

15 Blackwood rejects *Romance*, a refusal that prompts JC to invite FMF for a discussion about its disposal and forces JC into closer involvement with its writing.

26 Enjoys Admiral Sir William Robert Kennedy's *Hurrah for the Life of a Sailor: Fifty Years in the Navy* (1901).

November

7   (Thurs) Finishes part III of *Romance* by this date, though the novel will preoccupy the two writers until next March. JC now looks forward to starting a short story, probably 'To-morrow', and catches up on his reading of *Blackwood's*.

15 Olive Garnett and Elsie Hueffer visit, finding JC very despondent about his work and troubled by gout.

December

3   (Tues) JC's forty-fourth birthday.

Christmas reading includes JG's now-published *A Man of Devon* and CG's *A Vanished Arcadia* (both 1901). *Romance* also dominates the Christmas season, with JC and FMF planning a working holiday on the novel. The JCs leave for Winchelsea on the 24th, though collaboration is rendered impossible because FMF swallowed a chicken-bone at his birthday party (on the 17th) and is incapable of working. JC later comments on the closing year, 'The last has been a disastrous year for me. I have wasted – not idled – it away, tinkering here, tinkering there . . . ' (to Meldrum, 7 Jan 1902).

1902

January

6   (Mon) On his return to Pent Farm, JC commits himself single-mindedly to *Romance*, expecting to finish it at the end of the month. The period from January until the novel's completion in March represents the high point of his involvement with its writing.

7   An acute financial crisis – insurance premiums fall due – forces JC to ask Blackwood for an advance and prompts a quarrel with JBP, who refuses a further advance on *Romance*.

11 Wells visits, reads parts of *Romance*, and offers to stand surety on another advance from JBP.

16 Still 'in a devil of a fix' with his finances (to JBP), finishes 'To-morrow' (*PMMag*, Aug [*TOS*]).

24 FMF stays at Pent Farm for a few days to work on *Romance*.

27 Delivers part of *Romance* manuscript to JBP and continues work on part IV.

February

3 (Mon) While in London to lunch with James Blackwood and Meldrum, JC hears of the death of FMF's father-in-law.

4 Still in desperate financial straits, he feels out the possibility of further advances from Blackwood.

25 Proposes to JBP that the latter buy out his life-insurance policy, to be paid off by future writings. JBP agrees, the first of many instances when he comes to JC's rescue.

During the month JC reads and responds to Wells's published lecture *The Discovery of the Future* (1902).

March

7 (Fri) In London, delivers the final portion of the *Romance* manuscript to JBP.

9 'Falk' has been refused for serialisation by *Blackwood's*.

10 Comments on Bennett's *A Man from the North* (1898) and questions his over-tenacious commitment to 'dogmas of realism'.

14 The JCs spend a weekend with the FMFs, no doubt celebrating the completion of *Romance*.

17 Prompted by FMF's suggestion, JC begins 'The End of the Tether', whose troublesome composition occupies the next several months.

23 Pays a Sunday visit to Wells.

April

2 (Wed) Accepts H.-D. Davray's offer to be his French translator.

15 Writes to FMF, 'I miss collaboration in a most ridiculous manner.'

26 JG pays a weekend visit, probably soon followed by FMF for a discussion about his work-in-progress, *The Benefactor* (1905).

May

1 (Thurs) Post-*Romance* fatigue accounts for slow progress on 'The End of the Tether'.

15   In London, JC is forewarned by JBP that *Romance* will require cutting before serialisation.
20   A first batch of 'The End of the Tether', due to begin as a serial in July, is sent off.
31   The Treaty of Vereeniging ends the Boer War. JC goes to Morley's Hotel to see Blackwood, who declines to buy the copyrights of *Lord Jim* and the unfinished *YOS*, telling him that he is a loss to the firm. On arrival home he defends himself in a letter to Blackwood: 'I am *modern*, and I would rather recall Wagner the musician and Whistler the painter. . . . They too have arrived. They had to suffer for being "new".'

June
6   (Fri) In London, visits Heinemann's, exercising his art in 'exploiting agents and publishers' (to EG, 10 June).
10   Reads FMF's monograph on *Rossetti* (1902), already seen in manuscript. Congratulates Constance Garnett on her translation of Tolstoy's *Anna Karenina* (1901).
11   JG is enlisted to hammer out a scheme with Pawling to alleviate JC's financial plight. Soon after, JG visits and makes him a loan.
19   Present financial negotiations mean that 'The End of the Tether' is 'all behind' (to FMF).
23   A large batch of manuscript and typescript of 'The End of the Tether' due for *Blackwood's* is burnt when a lamp overturns; the material will need to be recomposed from memory. (Najder, p. 283, justifiably casts doubt on the amount of copy purportedly destroyed.)
25   JC compliments Meldrum on his *The Conquest of Charlotte* (1902), now ending as a serial in *Blackwood's*.
26   Proposes to minimise the effects of the recent fire by writing 4000 words by 2 July. Coincidentally, Gosse organises long-term financial aid for JC and receives a letter of support from James, who describes JC's work as 'of the sort greeted more by the expert and the critic than (as people say), by the man in the street'.

July
11   (Fri) JC gratefully acknowledges receipt of £300 from the Royal Literary Fund.
16   After visiting Winchelsea and with much help from FMF, he at last sends off the second instalment of 'The End of the Tether'.

August

5 (Tues) The JCs arrive home after some days at Winchelsea with the FMFs.

18 Visits Hallam Murray to deposit the manuscript of JG's *The Island Pharisees*, which Murray later rejects.

28 JG pays a visit. JC writes to EG that Wells brought Shaw to visit some months ago 'and I nearly bit him' – otherwise, no visitors except 'buzzing flies, fine large wasps'.

September

4 (Thurs) *Typhoon* first issued in book form by Putnam's (New York).

During the month JC toils at 'The End of the Tether', also revising the story for forthcoming book publication. The illness of Borys at the end of the month delays progress. JC finds time to read the manuscript of Elsie Hueffer's *Margaret Hever* (1909).

October

(Thurs) JC at Winchelsea, where, with FMF's help and after working three nights without sleep, he finishes 'The End of the Tether' (*Blackwood's*, July–Dec [*YOS*]). The JCs return home by the 21st.

17 Plans to read EG's *The Art of Winifred Matthews* (1902).

19 Venezuelan revolution results in blockade by Britain, Germany and Italy.

23 'Nostromo' first mentioned as a possible title for a short story.

c.25 The JCs go to London for a week's break, staying with the JGs at 4 Lawrence Mansions, Chelsea. There JC meets Meldrum, James Blackwood and other friends; he also sits for a portrait by Georg Sauter, JG's brother-in-law.

November

5 (Wed) After returning from London on the 3rd, JC finishes revising proofs of 'The End of the Tether' and informs Blackwood that 'the story is properly finished as originally contemplated'. He will soon begin correcting the manuscript of Elsie Hueffer's translation of Maupassant (*Stories from Maupassant*, 1903), to which FMF contributes a preface.

6 Writes to Bennett about the latter's *Anna of the Five Towns* (1902). A letter to JG refers to a 'forthcoming concert in Chislehurst [Kent]' (some time after the 10th) with the JGs.

13 *YOS* published by Blackwood (by McClure, Phillips in America, 8 Feb 1903).

26   JC and FMF have spent four days and a night shortening
      Romance to improve its chances of serialisation. JC returns
      temporarily to *The Rescue*.

December
3   (Wed) JC's forty-fifth birthday.
19   Meldrum writes to Blackwood that he considers YOS 'to
      be the most notable book we have published since George
      Eliot'. Two days later JC hears of Gissing's high praise for
      the volume.
22   Discontented as the year approaches its end, he complains
      to JG of 'Nothing done' recently. Sends Fenimore Cooper's
      'Leatherstocking Tales' to EG's son David for Christmas,
      thanking EG for his *Academy* review of 'Heart of Darkness'.
23   The JCs leave for Winchelsea to spend Christmas with the
      FMFs, where James is a seasonal visitor. There, perhaps with
      FMF's advice, JC sets aside *The Rescue* and begins what will
      turn out to be his largest canvas, *Nostromo*.
31   Writes to FMF's mother about how much the 'bond of
      genuine friendship' with her son means to him.

                              1903

January
1   (Thurs) Returns home feeling seedy, though looking forward
      to a visit from JG.
2   Sends *The Rescue* to FMF for his help and book-surgery,
      perhaps also symbolically clearing the ground for *Nostromo*,
      which dominates the coming year and beyond. At this stage,
      however, JC compares the story to YOS and sees it as some-
      thing 'silly and saleable' (to FMF).
5   Contractual negotiations for *Nostromo*, now seen as a 35,000-
      word story to be finished at the end of the month, have already
      begun.
9   JC's response to a questionnaire on 'The Books of my
      Childhood' [CDAUP] appears in *T.P.'s Weekly* (he refers to
      Hugo, Grimm, Hans Christian Andersen and Edward Lear).
16   The FMFs arrive at Pent Farm for the weekend to hold a
      joint birthday party for Borys Conrad and Christina Hueffer.
      During the next fortnight the first of the year's many bouts

of depression and illness occurs, with FMF invited to cheer up JC.

February

4 (Wed) Resumes work on *Nostromo*, though still 'low mentally' (to JBP).
6 Anticipates FMF's help should any crisis arise with *Nostromo*, a possibility that sustains him during the coming year. A synopsis of the novel is now prepared for Harper's and copy promised for June.
11 Meets FMF at Gatti's before both visit JBP and Heinemann.
26 Has read Clifford's *A Free Lance of Today* (1903).
28 *Romance* is accepted for publication in Britain by Smith, Elder.

March

2 (Mon) On a short visit to see FMF about this time JC is afflicted by severe gout and forced to remain at Winchelsea for the next fortnight under medical treatment and at a low ebb. Returns home on the 16th.
17 Still poorly and now under pressure from his banker, JC asks JBP to 'subsidise' *Nostromo*, envisaged as a story of 75,000 words to be finished in three months.
23 Again back at work, JC asks FMF to send him Dumas's edition of *Mémoires de Garibaldi* (1860).
27 Batches of *Romance* proofs begin to arrive, on which JC and FMF will work on and off until early September.
31 The JCs meet the FMFs and Olive Garnett at Hythe for the day. The two writers talk business, JBP having visited JC the night before.

April

2 (Thurs) 'My work is greatly crippled' (to JG).
21 FMF comes to discuss *Romance* proofs, with JG invited for the coming weekend.
22 *TOS* published by Heinemann (in America as *Falk, Amy Foster, To-morrow – Three Stories* by McClure, Phillips, Oct 1903).
24 FMF, Olive Garnett and JC meet in Gatti's, where they drink to the health of the new volume.

May

5 (Tues) Clifford brings JC to lunch with George Harvey (of Harper's) to discuss publication rights to *Nostromo*.

7   Presses JBP to pursue the Harper connection and sees him in London next day.
9   Invites CG to discuss *Nostromo*; the former probably suggests a course of South American reading which includes work by G.F. Masterman, Ramon Páez and Edward B. Eastwick.
13 Now virtually accepted by Harper's, *Nostromo* is described as 'contemptible bosh' and '*not a quarter* yet is written' (to EG).
20 Sees EG in London.
21 JC is unenthusiastic about Marcelle Tinayre's *La Maison du péché* (1903).
22 Interviewed by Clifford for an article in the *North American Review* (June 1904).

June
4   (Thurs) Now exceeding its anticipated limits, 'Nostromo grows; grows against the grain by dint of distasteful toil' (to JG). Borys is ill in bed.
14 Accepts an invitation from Clifford, perhaps to lunch at the Wellington Club with admirers of his work.
16 Sees JBP in London.

July
?4 (or 11) (Sat) JC passes on to Wells a copy of Richard Garnett's *The Twilight of the Gods and Other Tales* (1903), which he has read and enjoyed.
7   Estimates that *Nostromo* stands at 23,000 words and, the next day, describes the cost incurred – he is jaded, suffers from toothache, and is 'dying over that cursed Nostromo thing' (to CG). Tiredness and demoralisation will intensify during the autumn and culminate in a minor breakdown in late October.
28 JC's first letter to William Rothenstein (WR) agreeing to sit for a drawing by the artist.

August
22 (Sat) Sends JBP roughly 42,000 words of *Nostromo* (part I of the finished novel), which is optimistically envisaged as half of the book and described as 'very genuine Conrad'. Despite feeling 'half dead and wholly imbecile' (to JG), JC works to promote JG's *The Island Pharisees*.
28 WR comes for the weekend to draw JC, probably also

meeting FMF. JC proceeds to put the artist in touch with JBP.

Work on the proofs of *Romance* is completed in late August or early September, with JG in attendance at Pent Farm.

September

11 (Fri) The 'atrocious misery of writing' *Nostromo* continues (to WR), seriously slowed up from now until the end of the year by illness and depression. In early September JC and FMF have a difference on what dates of composition should be placed at the end of *Romance*.

19 First of three letters to Wells about his mixed response to *Mankind in the Making;* later in the year he reads another Wells work, *Twelve Stories and a Dream* (both 1903).

26 Gout and severe depression leave him at a low ebb for the next three weeks.

October

1 (Thurs) Still unable to shake off 'horrible mental depression' (to Elsie Hueffer), JC finds some consolation in the forthcoming publication of *Romance*.

3 JG invited to come and cheer up an ailing JC.

?7 (or 14) Just emerging from the 'hole' and harassed by debts, JC writes optimistically to JBP of an uncorrected manuscript draft of part II of *Nostromo* and reports that part III now occupies his mind.

16 *Romance* published by Smith, Elder (by McClure, Phillips in America, 2 May 1904; unserialised).

27 Now staying with the FMFs at Winchelsea, JC returns home on 2 November.

November

3 (Tues) Revolution in Colombian Panama leads to US–Panama treaty, by which time JC has probably met S.P. Triana, Colombian ambassador to Spain and Britain.

?4 With forced cheerfulness assures JBP that *Nostromo* will be finished by Christmas, though soon after complains of toothache and writes ominously to FMF, 'The end of all things is not far off for me' (early Nov).

14 A gift of £150 arrives from J.M. Barrie.

19 Has finished reading Bennett's *Leonora* (1903).

30 Further illness and demoralisation arrive at the end of
    the month, leaving JC 'beastly ill' and in bed (to JG).

December
 1 (Tues) Now back in England, Casement is invited – but
    cannot come – for a visit.
 3 JC's forty-sixth birthday.
 5 *Nostromo* amounts to 566 pages of manuscript, only twenty
    pages away from the fragment written in FMF's hand (see
    1904).
 9 Still suffering the effects of gout, JC works with little
    enthusiasm: he describes himself as 'run down – stale'
    (to JBP).
17 Reads E.D. Morel's pamphlet on *The Congo Slave State* (1903);
    four days later in response to Casement, JC expresses sym-
    pathy with the anti-Leopold movement but declines to join
    formally.
26 Has read CG's *Hernando de Soto* (1903). Writes to FMF's
    mother, wondering 'whether the collaboration is good for
    Ford?'
31 A 'disastrous' year, JC exclaims in a letter to Barrie, whose
    The Little White Bird (1902) he has read.

1904

January
 3 (Sun) Casement spends the day at Pent Farm.
 8 (or 15) In London to see JG, whom he promises to meet
    at an international 'festivity' on the following Monday.
17 Partly to seek medical advice for Jessie and partly to be near
    FMF, who has moved to London, JC and the family take up
    residence for two months at 17 Gordon Place, Kensington,
    where they are also near-neighbours of the Lucases.
23 Jessie has recently injured both legs in a serious fall, the
    beginning of a permanent disability.
29 Serialisation of *Nostromo* begins in *T.P.'s Weekly*.
This London stay represents the high point of JC's dependency
on FMF at a time when financial pressures demand that he should
produce quick saleable copy and growing despondency prevents
him from doing so. With FMF's help, he will also begin to play

the Indian juggler and commit himself to several competing projects: *Nostromo* engages him during the day; a new project of composing semi-autobiographical essays (later collected in *Mirror*) involves dictation to FMF at night; while he also finds time (again with FMF) to put together a one-act play. During these two months FMF may also have composed – or perhaps merely acted as scribe for – a section of *Nostromo* (manuscript pages 588–603; a fragment of part II, ch. 5) when JC is, according to FMF's later account, afflicted by gout and nervous depression. The section in question appears in *T.P.'s Weekly* on 9 April.

February

4   (Thurs) The Russo-Japanese War begins.
6   JC's bank, Watson and Co, collapses, leaving him with the prospect of paying off a £200 overdraft.
7   After consultations with Sidney Colvin and with much help from FMF, JC has written a one-act play, *One Day More*, a dramatisation of 'To-morrow', probably finished by this date (*English Review*, Aug 1913). Soon the play is send to Bennett and Beerbohm Tree (for his official verdict). About this time negotiations begin for placing the *Mirror* papers, now to be composed in tandem with *Nostromo*.
13   Attends a FMF literary party at 10 Airlie Gardens, with guests including Hudson, James and JG. There Olive Garnett hears him announce, 'I am at the top of the tree', to which James replies, 'I am a crushed worm.'
17   Associates himself with the Henley Memorial commemoration.

In late February or early March he begins reading Kazimierz Waliszewski's *Ivan le terrible* (1904).

March

2   (Wed) Finishes 'A Glance at Two Books' (*T.P.'s Weekly*, 1 Aug 1925 [*LE*]) on JG's *The Island Pharisees* and Hudson's *Green Mansions* (both 1904).
4   A homesick Jessie returns to Pent Farm, leaving JC in London.
7   Apparently under doctor's orders, JC goes for a two-day break to the Royal Hotel in Deal with FMF.
15   Mounting pressures over the last two months lead him to

feel that 'I am nearly out of my mind with worry and work. My nerves are all to pieces' (to Krieger).

20 Now back at Pent Farm, he nurses Jessie, who is advised by doctors to remain in bed for three weeks with her knee ailment and heart trouble.

21 A bout of influenza sends JC to his sick-bed.

27 JG comes to visit and offers help with revising the *Nostromo* manuscript. Mounting medical bills force JC to ask both JBP and JG for additional funds.

By the end of the month JC has probably completed six *Mirror* essays: 'Landfalls and Departures' (*PMMag*, Jan 1905), 'Emblems of Hope' (*PMMag*, Feb 1905), 'The Fine Art' (*PMMag*, Apr 1905), 'The Weight of the Burden' (*Harper's Weekly*, 17 June 1905), 'Overdue and Missing' (*Daily Mail*, 8 Mar and 16 Nov), and 'The Grip of the Land' (*Daily Mail*, 2 Dec). He now turns exclusively to *Nostromo* and will later report to FMF that 'almost full half of that book has been written in 5 months. From end Mch to end Aug^{st}' (22 Nov 1904).

April

5 (Tues) By this date JC has secured, through JBP, the secretarial services of Lilian Hallowes, who will remain with him for 20 years. At present, he feels himself in the toils of a 'horrible nightmare' (to JG): Jessie's illness, financial difficulty and gout have left him on 'the verge of insanity' (to Meldrum).

14 In London to lunch with Harvey, stays overnight with WR, whose pictures he goes to see at a New English Arts Club exhibition; next day he lunches with JG.

24 Finishes part II of *Nostromo*.

May

4 (Wed) Refuses an invitation from Unwin to attend a Royal Literary Fund dinner.

?7 Sends a first batch of *Nostromo*, part III, in corrected typescript to JBP.

16 Has started work on a preface [*NLL*] to Ada Galsworthy's translation of Maupassant (*Yvette and Other Stories*, 1904), which he finishes in June.

17 A suggestion by Pawling that JC and CG collaborate on an article comes to nothing, though the original offer – from the editor of *World's Work* – is taken up by JC alone.

25 In London, where he tries to see Pawling.
29 Pressed by FMF, now in the early stages of a nervous
    breakdown, to repay his £100 debt, JC acknowledges that the
    two writers should share the payment for *Mirror* papers.

June
 8 (Wed) WR sees JC and finds him 'in a very bad state of mind'
    (to Newbolt, 9 June). About this time WR begins an effort to
    secure financial assistance for JC, moving to get him a Royal
    Literary Fund award. As a result of WR's efforts, he receives
    a sum of £200 two days later.
26 Now preparing for the final drive on *Nostromo*, JC enjoys a
    Sunday visit from CG when the two have a joint reading of
    Mérimée's *Le Chat maigre* (1879).
27 Again back at work he laments, 'I am tired, tired, as if I had
    lived a hundred years' (to WR).

July
 2 (Sat) Reads Hudson's 'The London Sparrow' in *Kith and Kin*:
    Poems of Animal Life (1901).
 6 Finishes 'Anatole France I. "Crainquebille"' (*Speaker*, 16 July
    [*NLL*]), a review arranged through EG.
11 In London to see JBP, looks forward to completing *Nostromo*
    in a fortnight. Another *Mirror* paper, 'The Faithful River', is
    far advanced.
18 JBP is angered by a public rumour that he keeps JC
    under stringent financial control. At this time JC keeps
    in close touch with Elsie Hueffer about FMF's worsening
    condition, diagnosed at the end of the month as a serious
    nervous breakdown.
28 Assassination of Vyacheslav de Plehve, Tsarist Minister
    of the Interior, an episode recalled in *UWE*.

August
 1 (Mon) Elsie Hueffer at Pent, asking JC to settle his debt.
 6 FMF departs for four months convalescence in Germany.
19 Prompted by JBP's complaint, JC formally denies that
    'Pinker deals harshly with Conrad' (to Gosse). A.J. and
    Ernest Dawson visit Pent.
27 The frantic build-up to the completion of *Nostromo* begins.
    After a tooth extraction the previous day, JC goes to the

Hopes at Stanford to finish the novel, the chauffeur-driven car involved in an accident on the way.

30 Finishes *Nostromo* at 3 a.m. and sends the last of the manuscript to JBP, probably returning home later that day.

31 (and/or 1 Sep) JC in London to see JBP. Based upon JC's own hectic letters, all datings at the end of the month are tentative and approximate.

September
For the first three weeks JC revises *Nostromo* for book publication, adding sections at the end of the novel.

3   (Sat) Dips into Mark Rutherford's *The Revolution in Tanner's Lane* (1887).

5   Encourages FMF to send correspondence on German life which might be published in Britain.

?14 The Hopes arrive for a short stay, followed by their daughter for a week.

19 Sends Elsie Hueffer a cheque as part-payment for FMF's contribution to *Mirror*.

24 Starts work on *Nostromo* proofs while also thinking of a holiday abroad.

25 JG invited for a Sunday visit.

October
7   (Fri) Serialisation of *Nostromo* ends.

c.10 The JCs depart for three months in London, where Jessie's knee will be operated on; to begin with, they stay at 10 Princes Square, Bayswater.

14 *Nostromo* published by Harper (by the same publisher in America, 23 Nov).

15 By this date finishes 'Henry James: An Appreciation' (*North American Review*, Jan 1905 [*NLL*]), possibly begun since arriving in London.

16 Dines with G.W. Prothero, who asks for a critical paper for *Quarterly Review*, a suggestion that probably prompts the forthcoming 'Autocracy and War'.

20 The JCs move to 99b Addison Road, Kensington, near JG.

21 The Russian fleet, on its way to the Far East, fires on British trawlers in the North Sea.

23 For the following week Borys is in bed with tonsillitis,

while JC begins post-*Nostromo* symptoms of lassitude (with breathlessness and gout), his mood not improved by the recognition that *Nostromo* has had 'a bad send off' from the critics (to JBP, 31 Oct).

24 Jessie is examined by her surgeon, Bruce Clarke.

26 JC's letter of protest about the conduct of the Russian fleet is published in *The Times*.

31 Nursing two invalids, he asks JBP for immediate funds. By this date finishes 'The Faithful River' (*World's Work*, Dec [*Mirror*]). Despite receiving 'magnificent letters' in praise of *Nostromo* (to JBP), JC now acknowledges that 'the public . . . will turn its back on it no doubt' (to CG).

November

4 (Fri) WR invited for dinner on the next day, followed by Elsie Hueffer for lunch on the 7th.

5 Sends *One Day More* for Barrie's scrutiny.

7 JC's guests delay the completion of a short story for a planned 'Benavides' cycle intended for the *Strand*, but not published there and later reshaped into 'Gaspar Ruiz'. It is finished within the next few days.

c.14 The JCs give a large dinner party before Jessie goes to the nursing home, with guests including Augustus John, Lucas and A.J. Dawson.

22 JC is again pressed by FMF to repay his debt.

24 After lengthy examinations Jessie's operation takes place, though not successfully.

30 Mounting medical bills force JC to borrow money from WR and others.

December

3 (Sat) JC's forty-seventh birthday.

11 By this date FMF is back in London from Germany.

14 Accompanies FMF to see Dr Tebb. Jessie returns on crutches from the nursing home.

17 Visits WR.

21 Recovering from gout and looking forward to a forthcoming Capri trip, he makes vague plans to return to *The Rescue*, reporting that FMF is 'here [London] and getting better', and is ready to help with the novel. *The Rescue* must not, however,

divert him from the 'new novel' promised to Methuen (to JPB).

Between September and the end of the year JC completes three more *Mirror* papers: 'The Character of the Foe' (*PMMag*, Mar 1905), 'Rulers of East and West' (*PMMag*, May-June 1905), and 'Cobwebs and Gossamer' (*Harper's Weekly*, June 1905).

1905

January

1   (Sun) Now preparing for a four-month sojourn in Capri, JC offers apologies to his creditors and defends his previous year's expenditures to JBP, before returning from London to Pent Farm on the 7th.

13 Congratulates Wells on the first serial instalment of *Kipps* (1905). The JCs depart for Capri (FMF seeing them off at Dover) on a journey rendered laboriously difficult by Jessie's invalid condition, which confines her to a wheelchair. After an overnight stay in Paris, they leave next day by train for Naples, via Geneva and Rome. On the journey south JC begins 'Autocracy and War'.

16 Arrival in Naples, where JC writes immediately to JBP for additional funds. Bad weather holds up the sea-crossing to Capri for five days until the 20th, when they reach the island in the evening and take up residence at the Villa di Maria.

In Capri JC hopes to take a break from financial worry and overcome creative frustrations, though both are exacerbated by a trip which turns out to be 'a mad thing' (to JG, 21 Jan) – expensive, poorly organised, and fraught with misfortune. JC completes 'Autocracy and War' on Capri, researches a Mediterranean novel, makes a start on *Chance*, but accomplishes little else – and appears to make no major commitment for the rest of the year. On arrival, one of their first visitors is Norman Douglas, a writer whom JC befriends and whose work he will help to promote; JC also meets Count Zygmunt Szembek, a Pole whose experiences in Naples contribute to 'Il Conde'.

22 'Bloody Sunday' in St Petersburg, when protesting workers are fired upon.

February

3   (Fri) Has read CG's *Progress and Other Stories* (1905), dedicated to him.

5   Writes the first of several apologetic letters to JBP, who becomes increasingly impatient with JC's expenditures.

23   Recovering from the effects of influenza and acute insomnia, he decides that 'Autocracy and War' will need to be revised in the light of recent events in Russia.

March

12   (Sun) Now attributing his 'languid' condition to the effect of climate and scenery in Capri, he writes to Davray, 'I have done nothing. Absolutely nothing.'

23   Learns that he has been granted £500 from the Royal Bounty Fund, with Henry John Newbolt and WR later appointed as trustees.

April

3   (Mon) Painful toothache drives JC to Naples for treatment, where, with the family, he visits Pompeii. Soon after, the JGs visit for a week.

12   Writes to JBP that 'This place is a curse to me', with three months 'gone to waste.' By this date 'Autocracy and War' is finished and sent to JBP, though a first copy goes astray in transit (*Fortnightly Review*, July [NLL]).

23   Learns that the English Stage Society wishes to perform *One Day More*.

24   An impatient JBP has baulked at JC's request for £120 to settle his Capri expenses.

25   Thanks and praises Wells for *A Modern Utopia* (1905).

May

1   (Mon) Urges Alice Rothenstein to arrange for £150 of the grant money to be sent.

5   Has by this date begun 'Explosives' (*Chance*) as a short story and a week later speaks of it as almost finished.

9   Reads FMF's *The Soul of London* (1905), already seen in manuscript. JC has awkward exchanges with him about the authorship of *One Day More*.

12   On leaving Capri he issues his forthcoming policy for the year to JBP: 'Short stories – is the watchword now.'

13 The JCs depart from Naples by sea for Marseille (where JC visits Robert d'Humières and MP) and, after a night in Paris, arrive back on the 18th.

21 Leaves to spend a few days in London, where he sees JBP and, on the 24th after lunch with Colvin, meets Newbolt for awkward discussions about payment of grant. Soon after, he is forced home by a gout attack which lasts several days.

31 Finishes tinkering with *One Day More* before the coming performance and by this date also completes 'In Captivity' (*Blackwood's*, Sep [*Mirror*]).

June
5 (Mon) In the first of a series of letters to Newbolt laying out his financial situation, JC resists the suggestion that he should declare himself bankrupt: 'I desire to avoid the most remote appearance of being the XXth century edition of Johnson's Mr Savage.' A sum of £260 allows him to settle his immediate debts, with the rest of the grant being paid in small instalments until April 1906.

21 Shortage of money and lingering gout prevent him from attending rehearsals in London, though he is present on the following two days. He has now acquired a tutor for Borys and a secretary for himself in T.F. O'Connor (until Sep).

24 FMF is invited (but declines) to see the play.

25 *One Day More* receives three performances by the Stage Society at the Royalty Theatre. The JCs attend the final performance on the 27th, when the author is greeted by Shaw. JC will conclude three days later, 'I don't think I am a dramatist' (to JG, 30 June).

30 Has just returned from a short visit to FMF in Winchelsea.

July
4 (Tues) EG sees JC and Hudson at the Mont Blanc, the former looking well. 'Initiation' is now finished (*Blackwood's*, Jan 1906 [*Mirror*]).

15 'Books' appears in *Speaker* [*NLL*]. While planning a paper on Lord Nelson, JC works energetically to promote Douglas's work.

19 Receives a copy of Newbolt's *The Year of Trafalgar* (1905).

September

5   (Tues) The Russo-Japanese War ends.
20 After a week in bed with gout, JC finishes 'The Heroic Age'
    (*Standard*, 21 Oct [*Mirror*]). Meanwhile *Chance* simmers on,
    but progresses haltingly. Visitors during the month include
    the Hopes and the JGs (each for four days), FMF and
    A.J. Dawson.

October

6   (Fri) Finishes a paper later divided into 'The *Tremolino*' and
    'The Nursery of the Craft' [*Mirror*], which he probably takes
    to London on the following Wednesday. Promises JBP that
    he will now devote himself exclusively to *Chance*.
*c.*15 Finishes 'Gaspar Ruiz' (*PMMag*, July-Oct 1906 [*SS*]).
20 A series of recent illnesses and depressions culminate in
    JC's feeling that he is 'fighting with disease and creeping
    imbecility – like a cornered rat' (to Wells). Has recently read
    France's *Sur la pierre blanche* (1905).
26 Jessie, now pregnant again, has a 'nervous breakdown of a
    sort' and will soon need medical advice in London (to Ada
    Galsworthy).
30 After a 10-day general strike in Russia, the Tsar's 'October
    Manifesto' is issued; two days later, JC says that he is 'greatly
    moved' by events in Russia (to Ada Galsworthy).

November

2   (Thurs) FMF has read the opening pages of *Chance*. Enthu-
    siastic, he bets JC £5 that it will sell more than 14,000
    copies.
*c.*10 JC in London, misses JG, and returns home with gout.
*c.*15 The JCs go to London and stay first at 36 Princes Square,
    Bayswater, where, about the 20th, Borys develops scarlet
    fever. They move to 32 St Agnes Place, Kennington Park,
    to be near the boy's nursing home.

December

1   (Fri) Meets FMF.
2   Now realises that Borys's illness will be 'a long and ruinous
    job' (to WR).
3   JC's forty-eighth birthday.
6   FMF presents an inscribed copy of his *Hans Holbein* (1905).

c.15 Begins a severe attack of gout, which lays him flat until
       after Christmas.
29   'An Anarchist', probably written before the recent gout
      attack, is finished by this date (*Harper's Magazine*, Aug 1906
      [*SS*]). At the end of the year JC receives financial help from
      JG.

1906

January
(Mon) Completes a short note entitled 'My Best Story and
Why I think So', choosing 'An Outpost of Progress' (*Grand
Magazine*, Mar [*CDAUP*]).
 3   Collects Borys from his London nursing home and accom-
      panies him back to Pent Farm, Jessie having returned the day
      before.
 4   Borys has a brief relapse and doctors are again called in.
11   By this date completes 'The Informer', probably written
      at the end of the previous month (*Harper's Magazine*, Dec
      [*SS*]).
16   Has recently seen James and also meets Wells on the 21st.
18   Begins to organise the *Mirror* volume.
31   Reads JG's *The Man of Property* (1906), which he wishes
      to review.

February
 4   (Sun) In London visiting JG.
11   Sets off with the now-pregnant Jessie for a two-month stay in
      Montpellier, arriving at the Riche Hôtel et Continental during
      town riots.
Whether the result of creative lassitude, or the urge to diversify
his energies, or a deliberate policy to rescue his finances, JC's
post-*Nostromo* period has so far involved him in a medley of
smaller endeavours – short stories, *Mirror* papers, journalism
and reviews. The past year therefore leaves him dissatisfied:
he is restless with the lack of commitment to a major work,
impatient with what he describes as 'loafing' (to JG, 9 Apr),
and is no doubt afflicted by such unfinished projects as *The
Rescue* and *Chance*. In Montpellier a new commitment emerges

in characteristically slow and erratic stages when, on the 13th, JC begins a short story ('Verloc') which metamorphoses over the coming year to become *SA*.

21 By this date 'The Brute' is finished, but probably mainly written in January (*Daily Chronicle*, 5 Dec [*SS*]). JC sends 13 pages of *SA* manuscript to JBP, though further progress on the new story is interrupted until 5 March while he edits and arranges *Mirror* for book publication.

March

5 (Mon) Still conceiving *SA* as a short story of 18,000 words, JC presumes that it may be completed with one more batch of manuscript.

20 By this date finishes 'John Galsworthy: An Appreciation', a review of *The Man of Property* (*Outlook*, 31 Mar [*LE*]), followed by a three-day pause.

22 Complains to JG of 'mental exhaustion', though he adds that he 'has learned to write *against* it' and now accepts agonising slowness to be part of his '*method* of work'.

28 *Chance* lies dormant, though he has been 'nibbling' at it (to JBP).

29 Has recently read FMF's *The Fifth Queen* (1906), which he considers 'a triumph!' (to FMF).

April

4 (Wed) Now expanding freely, *SA* also becomes 'a damnably complicated job' (to JBP).

16 The JCs leave Montpellier and arrive home two days later. Proofs of *Mirror* demand attention for the next two weeks.

May

Having seen FMF during the first part of the month at the National Liberal Club and read his recent *The Heart of the Country* (1906), JC takes the family to stay at the Bungalow, FMF's temporarily unoccupied house at Winchelsea, from the 11th (Fri) to the 23rd. FMF visits at weekends, when the two men work on a 'larky collaboration' (FMF to Elsie Hueffer, 17 May) in the form of *The Nature of a Crime* (*English Review*, Apr–May, 1909). JC benefits from FMF's help with *SA*, as he had with similar subject-matter in 'The Informer'. Probably during this stay he first meets Arthur

Marwood, who becomes a close friend and, some years later, will be addressed as 'the real Wise Man of the Age' (to Marwood, 30 Apr 1915). For Jessie's version of this visit, see *JCC*, pp. 112–16.

31 Anarchist bombings occur in Madrid during the composition of *SA*. One of the sources for the novel, Sir Robert Anderson's *Sidelights on the Home Rule Movement*, is published this month.

June

?4 (Mon) After nursing Borys through a recent illness JC returns to *SA*, of which he has written almost a third.

24 The JCs now make plans for the birth of their second child, which will involve a move to London next month. Attempts to lend out Pent Farm to Tebb and WR fall through.

July

4 (Wed) Lumbago prevents JC from running up to London.

10 In readiness for Jessie's confinement, the JCs leave for 14 Addison Road, Kensington, lent to them by the JGs. During the two-month stay JC continues to work on *SA*.

August

2 (Thurs) Birth of the JCs' second son, John Alexander, named after JG.

15 Jessie and the new baby flourish, though JC's own position breeds Sisyphean gloom: 'I roll and roll and don't seem to gain an inch up the slope' (to JG).

September

2 (Sun) The JCs return to Pent Farm on or by this date.

7 The JGs call to see the new baby on their way back from France; JG has been reading the *SA* manuscript.

8 CG's wife Gabriela dies.

12 JC estimates that he has written 45,000 words of *SA*.

15 Responds with mixed feelings to Wells's *In the Days of the Comet* (1906) and fears that Wells may not like his criticisms.

19 Now prepares for his final drive with *SA*.

25 Attends opening of JG's *The Silver Box* at the Court Theatre,

where he also sees EG, Wells and Hudson, and stays overnight with the JGs.

October

4   (Thurs) Publication of *Mirror* by Methuen (by Harper in
    America simultaneously). Domestic difficulties delay the
    completion of *SA*, now accepted for book publication in
    Britain by Methuen.
6   Serialisation of *SA* begins in *Ridgway's: A Militant Weekly
    for God and Country* (US) and concludes on 12 January 1907.
9   Kipling sends an enthusiastic letter about *Mirror*.
FMF stays overnight in mid-October and asks JC to settle
his long-standing debt. The latter now works intensively to
finish *SA*.

November

1   (Thurs) JC receives an effusive letter from James about
    Mirror.
2   Finishes *SA* for serialisation, though it will require expanding
    and much rewriting for book version (see 1907).
8   Has read Wells's *The Future in America* (1906).
17 Reads and offers a lengthy critique of EG's *The Breaking
    Point* (1907).
15 Post-*SA* fatigue deepens into a depression which will soon
    send JC off to Montpellier in search of winter sunshine.
?25 (or 2 Dec) Reads the manuscript of JG's *The Country House*
    (1907).
27 Expects to be in London and to see EG.

December

3   (Mon) JC's forty-ninth birthday.
4   Completes 'Il Conde' (*Cassell's Magazine*, Aug 1908 [*SS*]).
10 JC in London (to see JBP), and again on the 14th, when
    he meets WR and Lucas, staying overnight with the JGs.
16 The JCs leave for France, stopping in Paris to see MP
    and Davray, and arriving at the Riche Hôtel et Continental,
    Montpellier, on the 18th.
31 JC has begun revising a French translation of *TU* by Davray
    and MP while also hoping to resurrect *Chance* as quickly as
    possible; he discovers an early France work unknown to him,
    possibly *Les Désirs de Jean Servien* (1882).

1907

January

Now emerging from the toils of depression, JC begins to respond to the change of scene and climate in Montpellier, though this interlude is only temporary and will later be seen as the calm preceding a storm. He enjoys some occasional reading, returning to his favourite French authors – Maupassant, Daudet and France. He also does research for his Mediterranean novel in the town library, takes Spanish lessons, and frequents the Café Riche (whose female orchestra is perhaps remembered in *Victory*). Meanwhile, *Chance* appears to lie dormant.

8 (Tues) Sends a copy of Théophile Gautier's *Émaux et camées* (1852) to FMF, to whom he reports, 'Work at a standstill. Plans simply swarming in my head but my English has all departed from me.'

9 Requests from JBP a copy of his 1904 review of Anatole France, which he wishes to send to the author.

14 Reads CG's *His People* (1906).

15 Declines to write a preface for an edition of Melville's *Moby Dick*, which he regards as 'a rather strained rhapsody with whaling for a subject' (to Milford).

25 JC at work on 'The Duel', an offshoot of his Napoleonic interests. A first round of family illness begins with Borys's adenoid trouble, which requires treatment.

27 The manuscript of Jessie's cookbook, *A Handbook of Cookery for a Small House* (1923) with a preface by JC [*LE*], is sent to FMF.

February

15 (Fri) Pacifies a growingly impatient JBP with promises that *Chance* will be finished by the end of the year.

26 Now revising 'The Duel', JC reports that Borys has measles and asks JBP for £15.

March

4 (Mon) Borys develops a mysterious lung infection variously diagnosed as bronchitis, pneumonia and possibly tuberculosis.

5 JC receives a copy of FMF's *Privy Seal* (1907).

13 Reports the need for a change of climate for Borys – a

stay in Champel, Switzerland – and appeals to JBP for help in financing it.

21 Accompanies two servants to Paris and picks up the family maid, Nellie Lyons, back in Montpellier by the 23rd.

April

8 (Mon) Recent stresses leave JC 'beastly ill without being laid up' (to JBP).
11 Completes 'The Duel' (*PMMag*, Jan–May 1908 [*SS*]), now hoping to return to *Chance*.
12 Has read the manuscript of JG's *Joy* (1910).

May

1 (Wed) Gout sends him to bed for the coming week and brings on extravagant depression; he has his arm in a sling and speaks of 'nervous collapse' (to JG, 6 May).
15 The journey to Switzerland begins, on the eve of which Borys catches whooping cough; he passes it on to his brother, and another harrowing round of illness starts.
18 From the Hôtel de la Poste in Geneva an anguished JC writes to JBP that baby John has worsened during the journey, the family is short of money, and that proofs of *SA* (not galley slips as he had asked) have arrived.
19 *Chance* is laid aside while JC, in the time left free from nursing his sons, corrects and revises *SA* for book publication. He writes an extra chapter and adds 28,000 words in all, a task from which he is not fully free until late July.
23 The JCs move to nearby Champel and the Hôtel de la Roseraie, where John and Borys can be isolated in an annex.
25 Further complications arise when Borys develops rheumatic fever and dangerously high temperatures.

June

1 (Sat) Suffering from gouty eczema, JC awaits funds from JBP to undergo water treatment.
6 At work on revising *SA* and nursing Borys, JC writes to JG, 'I seem to move, talk, write in a sort of quiet nightmare that goes on and on.'

15   The FMFs' offer to come to Switzerland is gratefully declined.
24   Borys at last starts to recover after four months of illness.

July
30   (Tues) Contemplating the family's recent ordeal JC summa-
      rises, 'a ghastly time, – from the 15th May to the 15th July'
      (to JG). Appeals to JBP for help with his chaotic financial
      situation and exclaims, 'No more trips abroad. I am sick of
      them'. He remains in England until his 1914 visit to Poland.
      Asks Wells's permission to dedicate *SA* to him.

August
 3   (Sat) Making the best of a bad job, JC pacifies JBP with the
      promise that he will finish *Chance* and 'another novel' within
      the next year.
12   Return to Pent Farm. The search for a new house begins.
13   Devises a pre-arranged budget with JBP of £600 a year (to
      start 10 Aug) on condition that 80,000 words of a novel are
      written in the coming year – a scheme that will increase,
      rather than lessen, pressures on JC.
15   House-hunting begins in Winchester with Harriet Capes,
      after which JC goes to London to see WR. By the 21st
      negotiations have begun for a house in Luton.
24   Reads 'a very interesting book on Rousseau' (to JG), possibly
      Jules Leamaître's controversial *Jean-Jacques Rousseau* (1907).

September
 3   (Tues) On his way to finalise negotiations in Luton, JC
      sees JBP in London.
 4   Lunches with Wells in Hythe.
10   *SA* published by Methuen (by Harper in America simul-
      taneously). The move from Pent Farm to Someries, Luton
      (Beds), begins. Just before departure JC and FMF have a row
      about JC's unpaid debts, which adds to his stress and causes
      a bout of gouty eczema later in the week. After a short stay
      with the JGs in London, the JCs arrive at their new home on
      the 12th.
20   JC sends a copy of *SA* to James.
27   Consoling JG on the poor reception given to *Joy*, JC enthuses
      about *Strife* (1910).

30   In London on a flying visit, he rushes home to meet
      the JGs.

October
1   (Tues) Responds admiringly to FMF's *An English Girl* (1907).
c.6   Stephen Reynolds arrives for a visit, soon followed by FMF.
8   Finishes 'The Censor of Plays' (*Daily Mail*, 12 Oct [NLL]),
      written at EG's request.
15   In London, JC misses FMF but meets the 'usual crowd'
      at the Mont Blanc (to FMF).
24   Informs JG (who has seen the *Chance* manuscript) that he is
      at work 'convulsively' on the novel, still his priority at this
      time, and hoping for a new-year completion.
29   At JG's request, JC joins over 70 signatories in a letter
      to *The Times* attacking theatre censorship.

November
3   (Sun) The WRs visit Someries for the day.
5   Spends the day with the Sandersons in Elstree before their
      return to Kenya.
      In mid-month, JC is cheered up by a week's visit from Colvin.
22   Returning home from a visit to London, JC is smitten with
      gout and in bed until the 28th; he complains of achieving
      little since August and laments, 'This trying to break through
      a stone wall is getting too much for me' (to JG, 27 Nov).

December
3   (Tues) JC's fiftieth birthday coincides with a growing frus-
      tration with *Chance*, now to be laid aside yet again. Perhaps
      on his birthday itself JC begins 'Razumov' (*UWE*) as a short
      story intended for inclusion in *SS* and anticipates a speedy
      conclusion.
7   WR pays a weekend visit, showing JC his forthcoming
      lecture to the Birmingham School of Art.
10   Attends a belated birthday party held for him by the JGs
      in London.
25   Reynolds spends Christmas at Someries. Gout afflicts JC
      from Boxing Day until 6 January but does not prevent work
      on *UWE*, now a 'more difficult job' than he expected (to JBP,
      30 Dec).

After sending JBP three batches of *UWE* in December, JC
watches it inexorably expand and complicate over the next two
years, while frequently anticipating completion and assuring an
impatient JBP that it is in sight. The ordeal of unshouldering
something that 'must come out' in *UWE* (to JBP, 7 Jan 1908) – a
prolonged trauma in itself – is further complicated by the financial
agreement with JBP that requires JC to produce 80,000 words of a
novel by 10 August 1908. By that date, he is not only held up with
the early parts of *UWE* but also commits himself to write for FMF's
English Review, a decision that will delay the novel even further
and sour relations with JBP, to whom he is already very heavily
in debt. Deteriorating relations with his agent are paralleled, in
1909, by a series of confrontations between JC and FMF which
results in a decisive break between them in July. Following upon
this loss of one of his closest friends and mainstays, and after
further tension between JC and his agent, JC severs relations
with JBP: upon delivery of the *UWE* manuscript in January 1910
they have a violent quarrel (which estranges them for two years),
with JC returning home to suffer a complete mental and physical
breakdown. Of the next two years he later writes, 'Here I've been
2 years writing a novel which is not finished. Two years! Of which
surely one half has been illness, complicated by a terrible moral
stress. Imagine yourself painting with the Devil jogging your elbow
all the time' (to JG, 17 Dec 1910).

1908

January
Early in the month JC issues wildly discrepant hints about the
size and scope of *UWE*. On the 6th (to JBP) he anticipates the
end of the story and expects it to be 9,000 words long; on the
same day he offers an ambitious synopsis (to JG); on the 7th *UWE*
is described to a presumably bewildered agent as a 'big machine'
and 'a reading of the Russian character' (to JBP); while on the 9th
he sends another batch of the novel to him, still believing that
Chance is 'the main thing'.

6 (Mon) Supports FMF's application for a Royal Literary Fund
   grant.
13 Takes a rare day off work with Borys.
16 After a meeting with JBP, to whom his debt now stands at

£1572, JC baulks at the financial guidelines laid down by his
agent and objects to being made to feel that he is 'begging'
for money.
As a means of protecting the integrity of *UWE* and meeting
JBP's request for saleable copy, JC deserts his new story in the
later part of the month and dashes off 'The Black Mate', written
in a week for quick magazine publication (*London Magazine*, Apr
[*TH*]).

February

13 (Thurs) Now recovering from severe gout and with 'The
    Black Mate' behind him, JC demands of JBP that he be
    allowed more financial leeway and a 'free hand' with *UWE*,
    whose completion, he still assumes, is not far away. He
    threatens JBP that, if the worst comes, he will finish *UWE*
    in French!

20 Recent visitors to Someries include Douglas, J.C. Tarver and
    Mary Martindale. JC has recently read FMF's *The Fifth Queen
    Crowned* (1908).

29 Advises Douglas on the latter's 'Isle of Typhoeus', later
    published in FMF's *English Review* (1909).

March

Temporarily rescued from last month's financial crisis, JC
proceeds to apply for a grant from the Royal Literary Fund,
sponsored by Wells.

11 (Wed) *UWE* is now envisaged as a story of 43,000 words,
    with JC having arrived at the end of part I and, on the
    17th, believing that he is at work on the 'last Chap.' (to
    JBP).

23 From this date onwards *UWE* begins to expand freely. It
    is for the first time called a 'novel(?)', and the question of
    its eventual title is raised (to JBP).

April

2 (Thurs) *UWE* now proves 'horribly difficult' (to JBP) and will
   continue to be so throughout the summer as JC struggles with
   a subject that 'has long haunted [him]' (to JBP, 7 Jan), writhes
   under financial constraints, and is forced into temporising
   with JBP. In the following seven months of gestation and
   composition he produces only 27,000 words.

10   Acknowledges receipt of £200 from the Royal Literary Fund.
21   Writes evasively to JBP, 'On the R[azumov] question I don't like to be positive.'

May–July
During the next three months JC attempts to mollify an agent increasingly impatient with lack of copy. In May he promises a June completion, even while seeming to realise that the story has 'run away': 'I can't let you have Razumov yet. That story must be worked out as it is worth it' (to JBP [May]). During early spring JC reads FMF's *Mr Apollo* and JG's *A Commentary* (both 1908). Progress on *UWE* is held up during June by revision and correction of *SS* proofs, and in July by a bout of gouty dyspepsia. July brings EG to Someries to see the manuscript of *UWE* but also another conflict with JBP over finances, probably after a meeting between the two men: JC adamantly refuses to be treated as a 'journeyman joiner' and wonders whether JBP will 'drop' him on their deadline date of 10 August (to JBP [Aug]).

August
6   (Thurs) *SS* published by Methuen (by Doubleday, Page in America, 15 Jan 1915).
18   Recent reading includes James's *A Little Tour in France* (1884) and France's *Jeanne d'Arc* (1908).
21   Robert Lynd's recent review of *SS* in *Daily News*, describing its author as a man 'without either country or language', annoys JC and may have helped to prompt *PR*.
24   Correspondence begins with Arthur Symons (another writer in the middle of a crisis), who sends the draft of an article on JC. The latter comments at length on the manuscript of JG's *Fraternity* (1909).
28   Now at a serious impasse with *UWE*: 'I have it all in my head and yet when it comes to writing I simply can't find the words' (to EG).
29   The JCs go to stay for the following three weeks near the FMFs in Aldington, where JC hopes to enlist FMF's help and do some 'heavy pulling at the novel' (to EG, 28 Aug). An idea originates during their conversations for a series of autobiographical sketches by JC (*PR*) which might appear in FMF's new journal, *English Review*. JC's added commitments, including his involvement with *English Review*, will seriously

hinder his progress with *UWE* and further antagonise JBP during the next 12 months.

September

18 (Fri) Having indirectly heard of recent complaints by JBP about him, a tight-lipped JC informs his agent of his new plans for *PR* (at this stage involving 12 sections), tells him that it will not delay progress on *UWE*, and demands his total support. By early December he completes the first four chapters of *PR*, including a draft of a story which will become 'Prince Roman', and a brief review of Anatole France – while work on *UWE* lapses.

*c.*20 Returns from Aldington, now impatient to move out of 'that damned Luton place' (to JBP, 18 Sep).

October

6 (Tues) Finishes reading a volume by Lucas, possibly *Her Infinite Variety* (1908), and also reads Reynolds' *A Poor Man's House* (1908) this month.

7 Offers JBP a summary of *PR*, describing it as an attempt to 'make Polish life enter English literature'.

13 Miss Hallowes finishes typing a clean copy of the existing *UWE* manuscript (up to part II, ch. 4).

From this date until July 1909, JC achieves a meagre 25,000 words of the novel. Its composition is now to be complicated by a simultaneous process of revision, particularly of parts I and II, which involves cutting 9000 words.

November

Early in the month the editorial group of the *English Review* comes to Someries, where the first number is substantially put together. JC is persuaded by FMF to write a last-minute review, 'Anatole France II. *L'Île des pingouins*', to fill the December issue [*NLL*].

3 (Tues) 'I have ordered my life badly', JC writes to MP.

25 After a recent break in London, JC assures JBP that he will devote himself to the 'last pages' of *UWE*. First issue of the *English Review* published, with JC much involved in its activities until next March.

30 JG reads part of the *UWE* manuscript while JC recovers from a recent gout attack.

December

3 (Thurs) JC's fifty-first birthday, with a visit about this time from Hope.

12 Acknowledges receipt of six volumes of James's collected works and rereads the preface to *The American*.

17 Tells FMF that payment for *PR* essays should be sent directly to him, and not through JBP.

Mid-month finds him issuing a spate of promises and hopes to JBP about a speedy conclusion to *UWE*, even himself seeming to believe that 'the end is just peeping over the horizon' (to Reynolds, 18 Dec). Another picture emerges after a further 10 days of gout and hard work when, left with an 'atrocious' temper, JC takes a more jaundiced view of his progress with *UWE*: 'But how long that bone will be sticking in my gizzard I cannot tell' (to Colvin, 28 Dec).

1909

January–February

The early weeks of JC's second year of struggle with *UWE* find him in sombre and apprehensive mood, harbouring thoughts of an early death (2 Jan), suffering from the effects of medicinal drugs (17 Jan), and feeling anxious and overstrained. The month is not unproductive, with a batch of the novel sent to JBP, who is told that '*Now every page tells*, the amount done being 75,000 words' (21 Jan). However, resoluteness soon gives way to stop–start rhythms of composition when JC becomes involved in moving house and later embroiled in FMF's domestic problems.

March

1 (Mon) During the coming week the JCs move to Aldington, near Hythe (Kent), occupying rented rooms above a butcher's shop. Given help and hospitality by the Gibbons, JC finishes the fifth instalment of *PR*.

9 Catches influenza and misses the opening of JG's *Strife*. New stresses now emerge upon the relationship between JC and FMF – the latter's high-handed mismanagement of *English Review* finances and contributors, and his marital problems.

29 The JCs have just seen JG's *Strife* at the Adelphi Theatre,

staying overnight with the JGs. Working on Douglas's behalf, JC sends the former's *Siren Land* (1911) to Lucas at Methuen. By late March JC is roughly at mid-point with *UWE* (the end of part II).

April

11 (Sun) The first of two crises this month occurs when JC confronts FMF on Easter Sunday and objects to his 'mania for managing the universe' (to Dr Mackintosh).

17 JC's recent reading includes J.G. Huneker's *Egoists: A Book of Supermen* and EG's play *The Feud* (both 1909).

26 FMF's marital problems (caused by his affair with Violet Hunt) reach a climax and involve JC when Elsie visits and implicates Marwood in the FMFs' domestic crisis.

28 A distressed Marwood visits to discuss the situation. Despite the month's turmoil (and the gout it brings on), JC finishes a sixth section of *PR*.

May

20 (Thurs) Defends himself against FMF's rebuke for not having received Willa Cather properly.

He manages to compose the seventh part of *PR*, though he pays for recent stresses with severe gout, which demands regular medical treatment from Dr Mackintosh. Like JC, *UWE* crawls along at snail's pace.

June

JC is again laid low by a severe attack of gout and depression, which brings JBP to Aldington on the 2nd and keeps JC in and out of bed throughout the month. He is unable and/or unwilling to complete the eighth part of *PR* for July's *English Review*.

8 (Tues) Has read CG's *Faith* (1909).

18 JG pays a visit, no doubt to discuss the turmoil in the FMF household, in which he too has been involved. Perceval Gibbon visits the next day.

July

3 (Sat) Receives a volume from Symons, probably *The Romantic Movement in English Literature* (1909).

11 Now separated from her husband, Elsie Hueffer visits to discuss the situation.

18 CG visits for the day, followed by Elsie in the evening; JC has been pondering JG's *The Eldest Son* (1910).
19 Afflicted by debts (now totalling £2250), JC has recently spent two days with the Gibbons.
31 Vexed by FMF's peremptory notice of his illness in *English Review* and his subsequent accusatory tone, JC writes an angry letter to FMF, marking the break between the two writers.

August
 6 (Fri) The JCs leave for a three-week break in Trosley (Kent) near the Gibbons.
With Gibbon's encouragement and access to his 'Russian notes' (to JBP, Aug), JC now launches himself on a more productive phase, and during the next four months completes the final 47,000 words of *UWE*. Meanwhile, Gibbon reads the existing manuscript of the novel.

September
18 (Sat) 'The Silence of the Sea' (on the missing ocean liner the *Waratah*) appears in the *Daily Mail* [*CDAUP*].
At the end of the month a visit from Captain Carl Marris, a trader from the Eastern archipelago, revives old memories and prompts JC to return to his Eastern material. *TLS* is later dedicated to him.

October–November
For the next two months JC works with sustained concentration on *UWE*, arriving at the end of part III on 19 November. Deteriorating health and morale accompany this last phase of composition. In October he reports to JBP an 'awful time during May, June, and July, what between disease, drugs, and worry', and in November suffers from a feverish cold and mental exhaustion, feeling that unless *UWE* is soon finished he is 'totally undone' (to WR, 15 Nov). A contributory worry concerns the JCs' maid, Nellie Lyons, who is confined to hospital with a severe illness.

December
 3 (Fri) JC's fifty-second birthday. About this time (partly in an effort to raise money to cover Nellie's medical bills) he breaks off from *UWE* to write 'The Secret Sharer' (*Harper's*

Magazine, Aug–Sep 1910 [*TLS*]), which he sends off to JBP on the 15th.

17 In a letter to WR, JC speaks of the agony and 'terrible moral stress' involved in unburdening himself of *UWE*; a week later he describes himself as a 'tormented spirit' (to Douglas, 23 Dec).

18 Another crisis occurs when JBP demands more regular copy, refuses JC an advance on 'The Secret Sharer', and threatens to cut off weekly payments unless *UWE* is finished within a fortnight.

19 Outraged, JC threatens to throw the manuscript of *UWE* onto the fire and responds angrily to JBP the next day.

23 The Marwoods, recently moved to Stowting, become near-neighbours.

29 *UWE* estimated at 130,000 words (to Gibbon), with JC now probably stung into finishing it as quickly as possible.

1910

January

12 (Wed) After recovering from influenza at the new year, JC sets about writing the concluding section of *UWE*.

22 *UWE* now finished. Then (or perhaps during revision in May) JC rewrites its two concluding scenes.

23 Colvin visits for the day.

27 JC delivers the manuscript of *UWE* to JBP in London. An explosive row leads to a two-year estrangement: he appears to be particularly hurt by JBP's cutting remark that he (JC) 'did not speak English' (to JBP, 23 May).

28 After staying the night with JG, JC returns home and, on about the 30th according to Jessie, suffers a complete physical and mental breakdown.

February

6 (Sun) Now prostrate, JC 'lives mixed up in the scenes [of *UWE*] and holds converse with the characters' (Jessie to Meldrum). 'Gout everywhere, throat, tongue, head. . . . Poor boy, he lives the novel, rambles all the time and insists the Dr and I are trying to put him into an asylum' (Jessie to Alice Rothenstein). For Jessie's longer account, see *JCC*, pp. 140–4.

9 JC's debts now total £2700.

11 According to Bennett, JC attends a Chelsea Arts Club dinner, though, given his condition, this seems unlikely.

For the next three months JC is confined to bed, allowed to see only members of the family and close friends such as Gibbon (a great support at this time) and EG, who visits in April. Though still in bed in mid-April, he is at last well enough to contemplate further pre-publication revisions to *UWE*. The world to which JC returns after his breakdown is much diminished, now lacking FMF, JBP and some of the close associates of the previous decade. Not until after 1912 will his circle really begin to expand and re-form, with the appearance of a group of younger friends and admirers – Richard Curle (RC), Francis Warrington Dawson (FWD), Józef Retinger, Bertrand Russell, André Gide and Jean-Aubry.

May

6 (Fri) Edward VII dies; succeeded by George V.

10 Still in bed, JC has finished revising *UWE* with Borys's help and promised aid from Robert Garnett.

17 A 'wretched convalescent', he now feels as if he is 'coming back to the world' (to JG) and looks forward to moving into a new house.

18 Begins 'A Smile of Fortune'.

23 Resumes correspondence with JBP, now addressed frostily as 'Dear Sir'.

27 Social life begins again with a visit from Clifford, recently returned from Ceylon.

28 FWD pays a first visit, bringing greetings from the Sandersons and Teddy Roosevelt in Africa; he also meets Marwood.

June

18 (Sat) Recuperation continues, with Marwood now a regular Thursday visitor. Has read JG's *A Motley* (1910).

21 Receives an offer to review regularly for the *Daily Mail*. JC accepts, but soon finds the task of reviewing popular books uncongenial and sustains the review column for only three issues.

23 Goes to the Gibbons in Trosley while the move to Capel House, Orlestone (Kent), takes place.

24 Jessie takes possession of the house, with JC arriving the next day.

28 'I feel like a man returned from hell', he writes to Douglas. A Writers' Memorial Petition sent to Asquith this month to urge the claims of a women's suffrage bill includes JC's signature.

July
13 (Wed) Edward Thomas has consented to ghost-write JC's *Daily Mail* reviews should the need arise.
16 The first of JC's reviews appears in the *Daily Mail* – 'The Life Beyond' (on Jasper B. Hunt's *Existence after Death Implied by Science*, 1910) – followed on the 23rd by 'A Happy Wanderer' (on C. Bogue Luffmann's *Quiet Days in Spain*, 1910), and on 30th by 'The Ascending Effort' (on George Bourne's *The Ascending Effort*, 1910) [all *NLL*].
31 Notorious mass-murderer Dr Crippen is arrested in flight to Canada. JC is asked (but indignantly refuses) to write an article for the *Daily Mail* on Crippen's reading material.

August
9 (Tues) JC is granted a permanent Civil List Pension of £100 annually.
10 Through Clifford's mediation, he has received an offer from the *New York Herald* to serialise *Chance*, which he now declines but accepts a year later. Receives a copy of David Bone's *The Brassbounder* (1910), read earlier in the year.
c.20 Thomas visits for a couple of days.
27 Helped by frequent visits from Marwood and Gibbon, an improved JC debates between *Chance* and *The Rescue* as his next project; he is now eager to settle his debts with JBP and dispense with him.

September
2 (Fri) Finishes 'A Smile of Fortune' (*London Magazine*, Feb 1911 [*TLS*]), then turns to 'Prince Roman' (a draft of which dates from 1908) and finishes it by the end of the month (*Oxford and Cambridge Review*, Oct 1911 [*TH*]).
27 Has read FWD's *The Scar* (1906).

October
Now begins 'The Partner', which he lays aside and finishes in early December (*Harper's Magazine*, Nov 1911 [*WT*]). For the next two months Douglas is in England and spends several weekends

with JC, who sees the manuscript of Douglas's *Fountains in the Sand* (1912). On one occasion Douglas brings Austin Harrison and Frank Harris to visit. Sanderson also calls on his return from Africa, while Harriet Capes stays at the end of the month. JC reads Reynolds' *Alongshore* (1910). October closes with the rueful admission, 'Nothing done to *Chance*' (to JG, 27 Oct).

November–December
Lack of purpose and energy makes the last two months of the year a dead period and accounts for 'three weeks in December without writing a line' (to JG, 14? May 1911). JC appears more interested in JG's *The Inn of Tranquillity* (1910) and Douglas Goldring's *A Country Boy and Other Poems* (1910) than in his own present work, 'Freya of the Seven Isles'. The militant phase of the suffragette movement starts with 'Black Friday' (18 Nov), five months before JC takes up *Chance* again. December sees the serial of *UWE* beginning simultaneously in the *English Review* and *North American Review*.

1911

January
For the next two months JC works on 'Freya of the Seven Isles', a story prompted by information from Marris. He also writes to EG of his post-breakdown condition, 'I feel as if I had somehow smashed myself' (12 Jan), anticipating a new and recurrent strain in his letters of the next two or three years: that he is past his best, tired with the uphill struggle of the writer's life, and has written himself out. This mood, manifested inwardly by 'nervous exasperation' with himself (to Douglas, 27 Oct) and outwardly by lay-off periods alternating with spells of wearily dogged composition, extends and intensifies over the next two years. After a visit to Capel House in 1913, Russell writes that JC 'said he had grown to wish he could live on the surface & write differently, that he had grown frightened. . . . Then he said he was weary of writing & felt he had done enough, but had to go on and say it again' (Russell to Lady Ottoline Morrell, 10 Sep 1913).
20 (Sat) Eulogises one of Wells's works, probably *The New Machiavelli* (1911).

February

5   (Sun) Agnes Tobin is introduced to JC by Symons, who takes the opportunity to read out his translation of Verlaine's 'Crimen Amoris'.

15   Marwood continues his regular weekly visits. FMF's *The Simple Life Unlimited* is published, with JC caricatured in the figure of Brandetski.

17   Supports W.H. Davies's application for a Civil List Pension.

28   'Freya of the Seven Isles' now finished (*Metropolitan Magazine*, New York, Apr 1912 [*TLS*]), after which JC hopes to take up *Chance*.

March–April

On 5 March enters a further period of creative dryness and persistent 'cold blankness' (to JG, 14 May), exacerbated by worry about Jessie's leg, pressing financial difficulties and threatening deadlines. Another urgent question concerns future secondary education for Borys, now 13. During this two-month relapse JC reads JG's *The Patrician* (1911) and the manuscript of EG's *The Trial of Jeanne d'Arc* (1912). By 28 March JG has stepped in with a loan. On the next day, having received a copy of FMF's *Ancient Lights* (1911), JC laments to FMF, 'Life – an awful grind . . . and yet [I] must go on spinning out of myself like a disillusioned spider his web in a gale.'

May

Makes a fresh start on *Chance*, writing 12,000 words in a fortnight. Treatment to Jessie's knee is put off so that he can press on with the novel, now being sent to JBP in small batches.

17   (Wed) In London, writes to Unwin that he contemplates collecting his *English Review* essays in a volume possibly to be called *The Double Call: An Intimate Note*.

28   CG pays a Sunday visit.

June

2   (Fri) Reads Hudson's *The Purple Land* (1885).

6   Borys takes the examination (unsuccessfully) for Tonbridge School. Soon after, in mid-June, the JCs stay with the Gibbons at Dymchurch while the drains are repaired at Capel House.

There JC catches a bad cold which he is unable to throw off for some time.

19 Has written 47,000 words of *Chance* (about a third) and optimistically thinks it to be half-finished.

22 George V's coronation. Soon after, JC reads Clifford's *The Downfall of the Gods* (1911).

July

8 (Sat) On receiving a telegram from FMF, JC summarises his present position with dismay – no published volume for three years (since *SS*), much 'savage exasperation' with himself, and spasmodic writing 'with long intervals of absolute dumbness. *Quel enfer!*'

17 Agnes Tobin and Symons bring Gide and Valery Larbaud to meet JC. Gide probably returns the following year and (from 1914) will supervise the complete translation of JC's works into French.

18 Reports to EG that he is 'pelting along' with *Chance* – though this momentum soon lapses.

28 Begins another dry creative season when life seems a 'dead pull' (to JG). This spell is not broken until mid-October.

August

1 (Tues) Marwood pays a visit, soon followed by FWD.

17 JBP's attempt to find a serial publisher for 'Freya' creates awkwardness between JC and EG.

12 Douglas turns up at Capel House with severe jaundice and high fever, and is looked after for a week before going to Ashford Hospital. He returns for four days of convalescence.

17 Tension arises between JC and FWD over racial issues in Gibbon's *Margaret Harding* (1911), a novel dedicated to the JCs.

24 Through Agnes Tobin, John Quinn contacts JC and buys the first of many manuscripts, starting with *OI* and 'Freya'.

September

The month opens with a week-long visit by Agnes Tobin, followed by a *New York Herald* interviewer.

22 (Fri) JC deposits Borys on HMS *Worcester*, a nautical training-ship at Greenhithe, where he will continue his schooling.

23 First of several complaints that he has done little work on
   Chance since midsummer – over half of the novel remains to
   be written in the next six months.
   Composes 'A Familiar Preface' for the forthcoming *PR*.

October
 5 (Thurs) *UWE* published by Methuen (by Harper in America,
   19 Oct), coinciding with the end of serialisation, after which
   JC is in bed several days with a cold.
15 Resumes work on *Chance* after revising *PR* for book edition.
18 Laurence Irving seeks permission to dramatise *UWE*, though
   nothing comes of this.
27 JC asks Douglas for a loan of £10, his 'nervous exasperation'
   at this time no doubt intensified by the first notices of *UWE*.
   Many reviews are respectful but unperceptive; some (including EG's) vex JC by their stress on the author's foreignness and
   anti-Russian feeling. Sales of *UWE* will be poor in Britain (only
   4112 copies in its first two years) and America.

November
 1 (Wed) Despite continual seediness, JC forces himself on
   with *Chance*, though with little enthusiasm – 'I am sick of
   the pen' (to Symons, 11 Dec).
 8 *Metropolitan Magazine* offers $2000 for 'Freya', a foretaste
   of the large fees soon to come after the popular success of
   Chance.
18 Reynolds comes for a weekend visit.
21 Suffragette riots in Whitehall, with 220 arrests.
30 JC's recent reading includes Henri Ghéon's *Nos directions* and
   Joseph de Smet's *Lafcadio Hearn: l'homme et l'oeuvre* (both 1911).

December
 3 (Sun) JC's fifty-fourth birthday.
21 Thanks FMF for his recent essay 'Joseph Conrad' (*English
   Review*, Dec).
23 Writes to Colvin about the 'lightning speed' of his 'hard
   work' on *Chance*.
26 JC's first extant letter to Gide, indicating that he has read
   the latter's *L'Immoraliste* (1902) and *Prétextes* (1903).
28 After a visit from Marwood the previous day, JC writes
   to EG about his *Lords and Masters* (1911).

1912

January

For the next three months JC works on *Chance*, 'writing MS. for dear life and in a sort of panic' as serialisation looms (to JG, 27 Mar). JBP seems to have provided considerable support at this time, and on 16 January thanks him for 'the conversation which has set my mind at rest'.

19   (Fri) PR published by Harper (in Britain by Eveleigh Nash under the title of *Some Reminiscences* at the end of the month).

21   *Chance* begins as a serial in *New York Herald*.

27   Colvin pays a weekend visit.

February

2   (Fri) Does not object to a visit from FMF and Violet Hunt, which they make soon after. Despite family illness, begins a final drive on *Chance*.

March

2   (Sat) Reynolds pays a weekend visit.

22   Completion of *Chance* held up by two days of illness and a recent visit by Reynolds and Gibbon. JC also visits Gibbon to cheer him up.

25   Finishes *Chance*. Goes to lunch at the Waldorf with JBP, a meeting which signals the end of their two-year estrangement. Then sees Harrison to try to persuade him to serialise *Chance* in the *English Review*.

26   The month closes with a visit from Marwood and an opportunity to read JG's *The Pigeon* (1912).

April

1   (Mon) After finishing *Chance*, JC is prostrate for a fortnight with a variety of ailments – depression, neuralgia and insomnia.

9   Has read FWD's *Le Nègre aux États-Unis* (1912).

14   Compliments CG on *Charity* (1912). Late at night the *Titanic* disaster occurs.

16   In London, JC attempts (unsuccessfully) to place a proposed article on the *Titanic* disaster with a New York daily. Eventually placed elsewhere, 'Some Reflections on the Loss of the *Titanic*' is finished by the 25th, when JC offers to be

at the Adelphi Hotel to read proofs (*English Review*, May [*NLL*]).

20 Visits WR in a London nursing home.

22 Still expecting *Suspense* to be his next major novel and also with plans to produce a sequel to *PR*, JC begins a short story ('Dollars') which will characteristically outrun its original limits to become *Victory*. For the next six months he repeatedly anticipates an imminent end to 'Dollars', not acknowledging until October that it is destined to be a full-length novel.

May

11 (Sat) Speculates to JBP that his new story may run to 18,000 words – even 30,000.

19 *Victory* is still 'simmering', though little has been written (to JBP).

27 Reads Constance Garnett's translation of Dostoevsky's *The Brothers Karamazov* (1912).

30 Sends a first batch of *Victory* to JBP. Recent visitors include Colvin and party, Symons, Hope, and John Mavrogordato.

June–July

Still conceived as a short story, *Victory* grows slowly, with JC now 'reading a lot' in connection with it (to JBP, 26 June). Towards mid-month he breaks off to write 'Certain Aspects of the Admirable Inquiry into the Loss of the *Titanic*' (*English Review*, July [*NLL*]). At the close of the month (when serialisation of *Chance* ends), he complains of a 'desperate futility' affecting his work (to JG, 28 June), anticipating the longer period of depression soon to begin.

August

13 (Tues) Purchases his first car, 'the puffer', a second-hand Cadillac; next day JBP visits.

18 FWD visits and reads aloud from his unfinished 'The Sin', which JC later helps to shorten; he invites JC to meet Lord Plymouth. St-John Perse, another visitor during the summer, meets Hudson and Symons at Capel House.

27 JC takes FWD to meet JBP, after which both to go the *English Review* office and then to FWD's Portland Place lodgings.

31 Thanks Reynolds for a copy of his 'Joseph Conrad and Sea Fiction' (*Quarterly Review*, July) and *How 'Twas* (1912), dedicated to the JCs.

Complaints about creeping illness and depression begin in late August and persist into the autumn, coinciding with a period of faltering progress. By late September JC describes his depression as 'awful – awful' (to JBP, 26 Sep).

September
3   (Tues) One of many predictions that *Victory*, now standing at about 30,000 words, will soon be finished.
20 The JCs visit the Gibbons and then proceed to the Hopes, returning on the 23rd.

October
3   (Thurs) JC feels seedy after four days in bed with gout.
7   *Victory* is described as a 'novel' for the first time and a synopsis is prepared for JBP, with assurances that the 'big' Mediterranean novel has not been forgotten.
12 J.G. Huneker pays a visit.
14 *TLS* published by Dent (by Hodder and Stoughton, Doran in America, 3 Dec).
20 Tea-time visit with FWD to the Embankment home of Lord Plymouth.

This month Max Beerbohm's parody of JC's 'The Lagoon' appears in *A Christmas Garland*.

November
2   (Sat) JC expects *Victory* to be finished before Christmas.
?3 FWD visits and finds Harriet Capes at Capel House.
6   First letter to RC, whom JC has recently met at the Mont Blanc and whose *Shadows out of the Crowd* (1912) he has already read.
7   *The Times* publishes JC's 'The Future of Constantinople' [*LE*], a letter partly prompted by Gibbon's departure for the Balkan War as correspondent.
17 Bennett contacts JC about a young Pole, Józef Retinger, who wishes to meet him. Retinger and his wife soon call at Capel House and become close family friends.
19 Attends a John Powell concert at the Aeolian Hall, staying overnight to see WR and EG. Gout cuts short his visit and

prevents him from attending Colvin's memorial dinner. Meanwhile, JC awaits a novel-competition which he will co-judge
with Bennett.

December

3   (Tues) JC's fifty-fifth birthday.
4   *Victory* has now reached 50,000 words.
6   RC pays a first weekend visit.
10 'A Friendly Place' appears in the *Daily Mail* [*NLL*].
23 By this date 'The Inn of Two Witches' is finished (*PMMag*,
    Mar 1913 [*WT*]). Work on *Victory* continues, with JC repeat-
    edly expecting to finish it soon – 18 months before actual
    completion.
Neuralgia and other ailments cause JC much pain over the
Christmas period and persist into January.

1913

January

15 (Wed) The JCs move to nearby Page Farm (until the 27th)
    while the drains are repaired at Capel House.
22 Despite painful neuralgia, JC visits JBP and Dent in London.
27 Still speculating about the completion date of *Victory*, he is
    none the less sure that it is 'nothing second-class' (to JBP).

February

6   (Thurs) Has read Jean Mariel's poems and essays, claiming
    never to have read a line of Goethe's.
9   JC's debts now reduced to less than £600.
19 Begins a running quarrel with Methuen over *Chance* and
    other long-term contractual obligations.
20 Anticipates both a new short story, 'the real Dollars tale'
    ('Because of the Dollars'), and the imminent completion
    of *Victory*; he also apologises for a period of 'diminished
    production' (to JBP).

March

16 (Sun) JC has shortened FWD's 'The Sin' (1913), which he
    now helps to promote.
27 FMF again requests repayment of JC's debt to him, now
    10 years old.

*c.*28 JBP brings JC to lunch with F.N. Doubleday, who broaches the subject of a limited collected edition of JC's works; Alfred Knopf will also pursue the project with him in July.

Family illnesses cause anxiety throughout the month, with Borys laid up in the school infirmary.

April

4 (Fri) Recovering from influenza, the JCs are visited by JG, who finds JC looking tired and worn; JC approaches him to be an executor of his will.

12 Fresh from reading MP's *Hors du foyer* (1913), entertains Colvin.

13 The Retingers and Gibbons invited for a Sunday visit; Douglas also spends the day at Capel House.

24 Visits Gibbon to explore possibilities of collaborating on a play. Meanwhile *Victory* progresses with painful slowness, now delayed by revision of *Chance* for the book edition.

May

3 (Sat) Again visits Gibbon to discuss their play – which comes to nothing.

17 Colvin and other friends arrive for the weekend.

30 Finishes revision of *Chance*, though rewriting lingers on into July, with an epigraph suggested later by Marwood.

June

1 (Sun) Describes *Chance* as 'the biggest piece of work I've done since Lord Jim' (to JBP).

2 Finishes reading proofs of Sarah Morgan Dawson's *Confederate Girl's Diary* (1913), edited by FWD.

20 Attends concert recital by Powell in London.

23 Back in London to see JBP and attend a meeting of the Fresh Air Art Society, of which FWD and John Powell are members, though JC neither joins nor agrees with its principles.

29 RC visits and is given permission to write a critical work on JC. Other guests at the end of the month include the Hopes and the Retingers.

July

12 (Sat) The JCs spend the weekend visiting the Gibbons and then the Hopes, returning on the 15th.
16 JC in London to see JBP and RC, whose study he further encourages.
22 Again in London to see JBP.
24 Finishes revising proofs of *Chance*.
26 Returns from a day in London and is now laid low by severe gout.
30 *Victory* is 'hung up again', with JC expecting to finish it in six weeks (to JBP).

August

2 (Sat) In bed for the past week and having written little for over a month, JC is gloomy and depressed but well enough to receive a visit from Lady Ottoline Morrell during the first week of the month.

With Marwood, he works on the manuscript of E.L. Grant Watson's first novel, *Where Bonds are Loosed* (1914), during midsummer.

September

2 (Tues) Again just out of his sick-bed, JC feels seedy and stale.
10 With an introduction from Lady Morrell, Russell has a first meeting with JC.
15 Is roughly halfway through *Victory* (651 pages of manuscript are with JBP), though the novel has been 'jammed for six weeks' (to JBP, 12 Sep).
18 Visits Russell in Cambridge until Saturday. *Chance*, due to appear in volume form, is delayed by a binders' strike at Methuen; some 50 copies survive with the original 1913 title-page.
20 Returns home for a photographic session with Will Cadby.
26 Visits an ailing Marwood.
27 Symons and Augustus John come for lunch, followed by RC the next day.

October

1 (Wed) The JCs to stay with the Gibbons at Trosley for a few days while Capel House is again under repair.
21 Another visit to the Gibbons, whose daughter is critically ill.

24 Has read the manuscript of FWD's *The Grand Elixir* (retitled *The Green Moustache*, 1925).
27 JBP visits when JC's gout prevents him from leaving home.

November
1 (Sat) Thanks Thomas for an inscribed copy of *Walter Pater* (1913).
6 The JCs read a draft of RC's chapter 'Conrad's Women' from his forthcoming study.
12 Work on *Victory* (of which roughly two-thirds is written) interrupted when John falls ill for two days and then by JC's decision to write a short story, 'The Planter of Malata': he will then 'go back to the novel with a better heart' (to JBP [Nov]).
13 FWD expected for an overnight stay.

December
2 (Tues) JC has read Larbaud's *Journal intime d'A.O. Barnabooth* (1913) and also some works by Élémir Bourges sent by Gide.
3 JC's fifty-sixth birthday.
10 Russell visits for lunch.
14 Finishes 'The Planter of Malata' (*Metropolitan Magazine*, New York, June–July 1914 [WT]) and immediately begins another short story.
22 Corresponds with Russell about the latter's 'The Free Man's Worship' (1903).
29 Writes to Colvin that 'we have all been victims of a mysterious epidemic which attacked us one after another . . . I have just come down after two days' seclusion. . . . A horrible Xmas.'

1914

The outbreak of the First World War in August serves to emphasise the two contrasting halves of JC's 1914 – the first centring upon the publication of *Chance* and completion of *Victory*, the second upon his return to Poland (his first visit since 1893), which coincides with the outbreak of war.

January

8 (Thurs) By this date finishes 'Because of the Dollars' (*Metropolitan Magazine*, New York, Sep [*WT*]).

15 Publication of *Chance* by Methuen (in America by Doubleday, Page, 26 Mar), which brings JC his first popular success and, from now on, a new measure of financial security. 13,000 copies of *Chance* are sold in Britain during the next two years.

16 Celebrates the publication with a week-long gout attack, which leaves him feeling seedy for the next two months and holds up progress on *Victory*.

New-year reading includes Symons' *Knave of Hearts*, CG's *A Hatchment*, and *My Life in Sarawak* by the Dowager Ranee of Sarawak (Lady Margaret Brooke) (all 1913); he also looks forward to reading Gide's *Les Caves du Vatican* (1914).

February

2 (Mon) JC in London to see JBP, after which he prepares mentally for a 'last long pull' on *Victory* (to JBP, 4 Feb).

21 Having now signed a lucrative contract with *Munsey's Magazine* (New York) for serialisation of *Victory*, JC pauses to contemplate its development and final title.

23 During this break he reads EG's *Tolstoy: A Study* and FMF's *Henry James: A Critical Study* (both 1914).

March

19 (and 2 Apr) (Thurs) Following quickly upon the exceptionally good press given to *Chance*, James's 'The Younger Generation' (on *Chance*) appears in *The Times Literary Supplement* – the only criticism to have 'affected . . . [JC] personally' (to Quinn, 24 May 1916). Still feeling seedy, JC contemplates the 20,000 words of *Victory* still to write and will soon realise that he cannot meet a May deadline.

30 Reads A.C. Bradley's *Shakespearean Tragedy* (1914).

31 Thanks Colvin for a copy of G.M. Trevelyan's *Clio, a Muse, and Other Essays* (1913), the essay on walking 'perfectly charming'.

April

25 (Sat) Looks forward to a visit from FWD who will soon rent a house near the JCs. Marian Dąbrowski's interview with JC earlier this year in London is published in *Tygodnik Ilustrowany*:

in it he confesses that 'something pulls . . . [him] to Poland'
(*CUFE*, p. 201).

May

5   (Tues) Has recently been in London to arrange coaching
    for Borys.
16 FWD visits and persuades JC to attend a luncheon in late
    May given by Walter Hines Page, who has been mandated
    to press JC to sign a contract with Doubleday, Page for
    a limited collected edition. Another visitor this month is
    Arthur Rubinstein, who has visited his native Poland the
    previous year.
27 The JCs travel to London and go to the Alhambra music-hall
    in the evening.
28 Attend Page's luncheon, where JC has a long discussion
    with Doubleday and meets Mrs Humphry Ward. The JCs
    meet the Colvins before returning home on the 30th.
29 FWD rents a farmhouse in nearby Ruckinge and sees JC
    regularly during a fortnight when the latter presses on to
    finish *Victory*.
30 The Empress of Ireland sinks, with the loss of over 1000 lives.

June

3   (Wed) JC and RC call at the *Illustrated London News* office,
    where JC reads proof of an article on the *Empress of Ireland*
    (published 6 June). Answering his critics, he soon writes
    another polemic on the same subject (*Daily Express*, 10 June;
    both combined later under the title 'Protection of Ocean
    Liners' [*NLL*]). During his visit to London he clashes with
    JBP on financial matters.

In early June JC accepts an invitation for the family to join
the Retingers on a planned six-week summer journey to Poland,
a trip which will coincide with the outbreak of the First World
War. Also in June, the first full-length study of JC appears, RC's
Joseph Conrad: A Study.

7   (or 14) FWD brings Ellen Glasgow for a Sunday visit to
    Capel House.
27 Completes *Victory*, with much revision and rewriting to
    follow in July, when its final title is also determined.
28 Archduke Franz Ferdinand assassinated at Sarajevo. Accom-
    panied by RC, JC goes with Borys to Sheffield for the latter's

university entrance examinations, beginning on the next day. JC dines with the Vice-Chancellor of the university.

July

3 (Fri) Stays with the Wedgwoods at Stonefall Hall, near Harrogate, returning to Sheffield for the second part of Borys's exams (6–7 July).

8 Arrives back in London, having the previous night seen George Robey perform at a Sheffield music hall. Returns to Capel House on the 10th.

*c.*20 Has a final meeting with JBP in London before the visit to Poland, which he now anticipates with mixed feelings.

22 Russell arrives for the day, eager to learn JC's professional opinion of his novella *The Perplexities of John Forstice* (1972).

25 The JC-Retinger party depart from Harwich for Poland via Hamburg and stay overnight in Berlin on the 27th.

28 Austria–Hungary declares war on Serbia, followed by declaration of war by Germany on Russia. The travelling party move from Berlin to Cracow, where, on an after-supper walk with the Retingers and Borys, JC has his first view of Poland for 20 years.

29 Two days of sightseeing begin in Cracow, with visits to the Jagiellonian Library, Apollo's grave at Rakowice Cemetery, Wawel Castle and the Cathedral.

31 Visit to Konstanty Buszczyński's country estate, Górka Narodowa. General mobilisation of Austria forces the party into a hasty reconsideration of its travel itinerary.

August

1 (Sat) While Retinger leaves for England, the JCs (with Otolia Retinger) decide to move to unmilitarised territory and the next day travel to Zakopane, where, after a brief stay at the Pension Stamary, they take up residence with Aniela Zagórska at her pension, Villa Konstantynówka.

4 Britain declares war on Germany.

Precariously cut off from England, JC will soon be faced with the problem of acquiring funds and permits to make the journey home without risking the safety of the family. Contrary to popular opinion in Zakopane, he does not think the war will be short and envisages it lasting for three years at least. Nevertheless, he is 'in a particularly equable and serene frame of mind' (*CUFE*, p. 211) for the first part of his two-month stay. Life in Zakopane allows for days of relaxed conversation, much of it 'connected with the war, and possible horoscopes for Poland' (*CUFE*, p. 244), with JC also writing a four-page political memorandum on the future of Poland. He enjoys meeting Zeromski and, through Zagórska, a course in Polish reading – in particular Prus, Wyspiański and Sieroszewski. He also sits for a portrait by Kazimierz Górski. The strain of being trapped and cut off without money in Poland begins to tell in September when JC, aware that he is 'destitute of means' (to JBP, 15 Sep), suffers a gout attack. Finally, with the help of JBP, Page and Frederic Penfield, the JCs receive (6 Oct) their permit to leave Poland.

October

8   (Thurs) They leave Zakopane for Cracow, where they stay overnight, leaving next day for Vienna.
10 In Vienna JC suffers from gout for four days and is laid up.
18 They leave Vienna for Milan, arriving the next day.
21 They leave Milan for Genoa, from where, on the 24th, they embark for home in the SS *Vondel*.

November

2   (Mon) Arriving at Tilbury Docks in the evening, the JCs stay overnight at the Norfolk Hotel. Next day JC sees JBP and Edmund Candler.
On his return JC is laid up with gout and arthritis, afflicted also by war gloom and a sense of his own physical uselessness which persists into 1915. He does not return to his writing desk until the 15th.

December

1   (Tues) JBP invited on this day.
3   JC's fifty-seventh birthday.
11 'Poland Revisited' appears to have been substantially drafted by this date, though revision and rewriting continue during the next few months (*Daily News and Leader*, 29 and 31 Mar, 6 and 9 Apr 1915 [*NLL*]).
25 The Retingers spend Christmas at Capel House.

1915

January

The 'sort of sick-apathy' which had plagued JC at the close of the previous year (to JG, 15 Nov 1914) continues into the early part of 1915 and accounts for recurring moods of lassitude and despondency which prevent him from working continuously. His indisposition brings both JBP and RC to Capel House at mid-month.

19 (Tues) At JBP's suggestion, he now plans to revive *The Rescue* and will tinker at it intermittently for two years (until Dec 1916). By this date JC's debt to JBP is reduced to £230.

28 RC having just left, JC writes, 'This war attends my uneasy pillow like a nightmare' (to Iris Wedgwood).

February

3 (Wed) By this date JC has finished revising proofs for the American book edition of *Victory* and has probably begun writing *The Shadow-Line*, which will progress haltingly through the year. *Victory* is serialised this month in *Munsey's Magazine* (New York).

24 *WT* published by Dent (by Doubleday, Page in America, 15 Jan 1916).

26 The JCs leave for a week in London at the Norfolk Hotel.

March

6 (Sat) Return to Capel House.

18 FMF sends a presentation copy of *The Good Soldier* (1915).

27 *Victory* published by Doubleday, Page (by Methuen in Britain, 24 Sep), JC later informing Colvin (28 Sep) of '11,000 copies . . . sold in the first three days'. Invited by Paderewski, JC declines to join the Polish War Relief Committee.

29 First meditates a film adaptation of 'Gaspar Ruiz', a project put off until 1920.

April–May

Complaints of physical and mental enervation recur from April to the end of August. Social life now severely curtailed by the war, JC keeps only spasmodic contact with Marwood, Gibbon, RC, JBP and the Colvins (whom the JCs visit at the end of April). Retinger, a more frequent visitor, interests JC in his plans to internationalise

the Polish question; JC visits JBP in mid-May and arranges a £50
loan for Retinger. Despite lumbago, he makes some progress with
The Shadow-Line and professes to have done a 'good bit' to *The
Rescue* (to JBP, 22 May).

June

1   (Tues) First Zeppelin attack on London.
16   Asks Unwin to send a copy of Lord Eversley's *The Partitions
     of Poland* (1915).
23   Collects Borys from Oxford, where he has been preparing
     for his university entrance examinations.
26   Having delivered a batch of *The Shadow-Line* to JBP, JC
     escorts Borys to Sheffield, where the latter successfully
     retakes his entrance examinations, though he decides by
     3 August to enlist in the army.

July

24   (Sat) During an uneventful and largely unproductive mid-
     summer, JC complains to James of his present meagre
     achievement, though he does succeed in delivering a
     further section of *The Shadow-Line* in early August.
27   Writes to the Royal Society of Literature that he is in favour
     of setting up a special committee to study the proposal (by
     Shaw) for a scientific alphabet.

August

6   (Fri) In London, thanks Colvin for a copy of his English
     Association lecture, 'On Concentration and Suggestion in
     Poetry', telling him that 'the only poem of Meredith that I
     passionately care for is the only one that I thoroughly under-
     stand, viz. Love in the Valley'.
12   Agrees to act as literary executor for FMF, who has by
     now enlisted in the army.

September

2   (Thurs) Sees JBP in London.
20   Borys leaves for army training, eventually to be attached
     to the Mechanical Transport Corps. JC in London.
27   Declines to speak at the Polish Association in London.
26   RC at Capel House for a visit.
28   Sees JBP in London.

October

6 (Wed) JG at Capel House, finding the JCs well.

8 On a weekend stay at the Norfolk Hotel, the JCs go to see Gounod's *Romeo et Juliette* at the Shaftesbury Theatre.

c.16 After another London visit, JC returns home with gout and is unwell until the end of the month and nursed by Jessie.

24 CG and Mrs Dummett, his companion, join a larger party at Capel House.

26 Estimates that he has written only 20,000 words in 1915.

28 Finishes reading CG's *Bernal Diaz del Castillo* (1915).

November

The effects of painful gout linger into this month, with a weakened JC confined to his room.

23 (Tues) He is over-optimistic in inviting JBP to come to collect the finished typescript of *The Shadow-Line* at the end of the month.

December

3 (Fri) JC's fifty-eighth birthday.

17 Finishes *The Shadow-Line* (*English Review*, Sep 1916–Mar 1917), three days before Borys arrives home on leave.

1916

January–February

Borys's departure for his unit (and soon for France) leaves JC lonely and cheerless, lacking conviction in his own creative potency – he complains to FWD that his 'mentality seems to have gone to pieces' (12 Feb) – and in the efficacy of all art: 'war stands in the way of abstract writing' (to JBP [1916]). As a release from such an impasse, JC appears to be more than receptive to the year's many diversions: trips to London and Southsea in January; a new temptation to dabble in the theatre when Basil Hastings makes an approach to dramatise *Victory* (6 Jan); the coming 'adoption' of Jane Anderson; and, later in the year, a connection with the war-effort in the form of naval tours. Meanwhile, the end of February brings the death of Henry James (28th) and JC's feeling remark the day before, 'I am slowly getting more and more of a cripple' (to Quinn).

March

10 (Fri) Goes to London for two days to sit for a bust by Jo Davidson, later bought by Gosse and presented to the National Portrait Gallery.

30 By this date 'The Warrior's Soul' is finished, though held back for some time (*Land and Water*, 29 Mar 1917 [*TH*]).

Plans for a collected edition of JC's work take a step forward this month when Doubleday suggests that Author's Notes should be written.

April

10 (Mon) Enjoys and admires Wilson Follett's *Joseph Conrad* (1915).

12 Supports Thomas's application for a Civil List Pension.

c.13 The bust of JC is unveiled at Davidson's studio, where Jessie meets Jane Anderson.

19 By this date Jane has visited Capel House. During the year she will seek 'to get herself adopted as . . . [the family's] big daughter' (to RC, 20 Aug).

21 Casement is arrested in Ireland and charged with treason. JC later declines to add his signature to an appeal for clemency. (Casement is executed on 3 Aug.)

24 The Easter Rebellion in Dublin. Karola Zagórska stays for a brief visit.

During this month JC prepares the text of *AF* for Doubleday's Collected Edition, with preparation of other novels to follow during the next two years.

May

13 (Sat) The death of Marwood, whose funeral (on the 17th) JC is too unwell to attend.

18 Symons visits for lunch.

19 Sits for WR at the latter's Ebury St studio. Negotiations with Doubleday continue, though publication of the planned Collected Edition is suspended until war ends. Meanwhile, JC interests himself in Gide's French edition of his works, though its first fruits – Isabelle Rivière's translation of *Victory* – do not please the author.

20 Cancels a house-hunting expedition with JBP to entertain Colvin for the weekend.

30 In response to FMF's request for repayment of debt, JC asks JBP to send £25.

June
In better spirits and improved in health, JC entertains W.H. Davies at Whitsuntide and later writes 'A Note on the Polish Problem' [*NLL*] at the request of Retinger for circulation in the Foreign Office. Walpole's *Joseph Conrad* is published, while JC himself revises *The Shadow-Line* and makes another half-hearted attempt to take up *The Rescue*.

July
1   (Mon) The Somme offensive begins.
2   Lord Northcliffe, on a visit to Capel House, befriends Borys and John.
12 Attends a British Academy lecture by Maurice Barrès, 'Le Blason de la France, ou ses traits éternels dans cette guerre et dans les vieilles épopées', at the Royal Academy. About this time JC may have had a farewell meeting with FMF before the latter's departure for the front on the 13th.
19 Provisionally welcomes Irving's interest in staging *Victory*.
23 Complains to EG of mental unfitness for serious work.

August
3   (Thurs) Meeting Hastings and Irving at the Garrick Club, JC pledges help with *Victory* and sees a complete scenario of the play later in the month.
16 The Polish memorandum is received at the Foreign Office, where JC and Retinger are subsequently interviewed.
The 'great void' left by RC's departure for active service is now partly filled by Retinger, whose political activities 'go on at white heat' (to RC, 20 Aug), and also by Jane Anderson, the 'pretty woman' whom JBP is invited to meet this month (to JBP [1916]).

September
4   (Mon) A busy month begins with a visit to see Sir Douglas Brownrigg in connection with propaganda articles for the Admiralty and a proposed programme of visits to naval bases.
6   At work on the stage version of *Victory*.
11 Goes to Ramsgate on naval inspection.

13	In London, where he meets Hastings and dines with Jane Anderson, before proceeding next day to Lowestoft to begin another tour.

15	Inspects anti-aircraft artillery in Lowestoft.

16	After lunch at Royal Navy Air Station in Yarmouth, JC departs for Lowestoft and a two-day tour in the minesweeper *Brigadier*, returning to Yarmouth on the 18th for a short biplane flight, later described in 'Flight' (*Fledgling*, June 1917 [*NLL*]).

19	Now back in London, JC meets JG and JBP at Romano's before joining Jessie and Jane Anderson in Folkestone.

26	Further naval tours take JC to Liverpool, from where (on the 29th) he departs for Glasgow. While there he lunches with CG.

October

1	(Sun) Leaves Glasgow for the Rosyth naval base, returning home on the 4th.

30	Completes 'The Tale', his only war story (*Strand Magazine*, Oct 1917 [*TH*]) and revisits Ramsgate.

November

2	(Thurs) Leaves home and meets Lord Northcliffe in London, before travelling north to Edinburgh to join one of the so-called 'Q' ships, HMS *Ready*.

6	The *Ready*, a brigantine disguised as a merchant vessel to lure out enemy submarines, departs from Granton Harbour for a 10-day mission in the North Sea; in the evenings JC reads Hartley Withers' *War and Lombard Street* (1915).

16	Arrives back in Bridlington (where, according to Jessie's eccentric recollection, he is arrested as an alien). In fact he leaves directly for the Norfolk Hotel, London, but, not arriving home until the 24th, is perhaps diverted by Jane Anderson.

25	Douglas is arrested on a charge of molesting a 16-year-old boy.

December

3	(Sun) JC's fifty-ninth birthday.

4	The present course of the war, JC explains to Dent, accounts for his 'inability to concentrate' on *The Rescue*, soon to be laid aside again until 1918. He does, however, manage to write 'The Unlighted Coast', though it is not published by the Admiralty (*The Times*, 18 Aug 1925 [*LE*]).

7   Reads Symons' *Figures of Several Centuries* (1916), dedicated
    to him.
10 (or 17) Recommends Jane Anderson's writings to JBP. The
    three foregather for tea at the Norfolk this month.
10 Thomas stays overnight before going on front-line service.
    He is followed by Hastings, who has now finished the stage
    Victory. At this time JC is also approached by Harold Brig-
    house, the theatrical producer, about a possible dramatisation
    of *AF*.
24 Writes to FMF on hearing that he has been gassed at the front.

1917

January
Borys, on a 10-day leave, celebrates his birthday at home on the
15th. When he departs, JC begins an unproductive six months
in which his total output amounts to three prefaces, two for
new editions of his work (*Lord Jim* and *YOS*) and one for a volume
by EG. Intensifying gloom and physical lameness lead him to
feel that 'I am still like a man in a nightmare. And who can
be articulate in a nightmare?' (to RC, 27 Mar). Though the stage
Victory is still a long way from production, theatrical plans and
tentative casting provide a welcome diversion.
30 (Tues) In London to see JBP.

February
26 (Mon) *One Day More* is privately printed, the first of 26
    limited-edition pamphlets to be published by Shorter and
    Wise over the next three years.

March
8   (Thurs) The 'February' Revolution begins in Russia; the
    Tsar abdicates. Later in the month JC writes, 'Can't say I am
    delighted at the Russian revolution. The fate of Russia is of
    no interest whatever to me' (to Dent, 19 Mar).
17 Hastings visit to discuss *Victory*. JC plans a wedding-
    anniversary gift for Jessie – a self-propelling wheelchair.
19 *The Shadow-Line* published by Dent (by Doubleday, Page in
    America, 27 Apr). Its first English edition of 5000 copies is
    sold out by the 23rd.

22 *The Times Literary Supplement* refers to *The Shadow-Line* as 'one of the great ones, not of the present, but of the world'.

23 JC is one of 15 members of the Commemoration Committee in honour of Sienkiewicz and Verhaeren, which meets today at the Aeolian Hall under the auspices of the Polish Information Committee.

26 Early reviews of *The Shadow-Line* provide only temporary pleasure. Lame and afflicted by the nightmare of war, JC informs RC the next day, 'I simply *can't* write' and adds, 'We are very lonely here. No one down for months and months.'

April

2 (Mon) A visit by Colvin arranged, apparently before the 21st, JC 'flying out against Gambetta'.

6 The United States enters the war.

9 Thomas, whom the JCs have seen only a few days earlier, is killed in the war-action. Preparing to sign a contract with Irving (on 3 May) for *Victory*, JC throws himself into plans for its casting. Other theatrical possibilities now begin to interest him: he toys with the idea of dramatising *UWE* and of collaborating with Hastings on an original play with an Italian setting about a faked old master.

21 Gide finishes translating 'Typhoon', which he will soon send to JC.

May

7 (Mon) EG stays overnight, with JC finishing the preface [*NLL*] to the former's *Turgenev: A Study* (1917).

14 Sees Gounod's *Faust* at the Garrick Theatre and (with Hastings) Irving's production of *Hamlet* the next night at the Savoy.

June

2 (Sat) Writes to the Paymaster General relinquishing his Civil List Pension.

July–September

The drift of the early half of the year is halted when, towards the end of July, JC begins a short story which turns out to be his first long work of the year, *AG*, also the first of his novels

to be largely dictated. In the same month, on a five-day leave
in Paris, Borys meets Retinger and Jane Anderson, and realises
that he has 'fallen heavily for Jane' (*MFJC*, p. 119). Despite poor
health, JC continues with *AG* throughout the summer, the routine
broken by visits to JBP in London and John's arrival home from
school. In September he reads JG's *Beyond* (1917), but the main
event of the month is Borys's return on a 10-day leave.

October
15 (Tues) Attends the centennial Kościuszko memorial meeting
    at Kingsway Hall.
21 Reads the manuscript of JG's *Five Tales* (1918) and informs
    him that he is 'half paralyzed mentally'. Five days later he
    laments that he is also 'dead lame' (to EG, 26 Oct).
31 Jessie's worsening condition will soon necessitate a move
    to London for surgery.
In this month JC writes the Author's Note to a new edition
of *Nostromo*.

November
7   (Wed) The 'October' Revolution in Russia.
12 JC starts reading Colvin's *John Keats: His Life and Poetry* (1917).
14 Lunches with JG at Romano's.
c.20 The JCs begin a three-month stay in London, staying first at
    the Norfolk Hotel. JC then moves to 4C Hyde Park Mansions
    to be near Jessie's nursing home in York Place. Amputation
    of a leg is averted in favour of physiotherapy, with a heavy
    metal splint being attached to her leg.
27 Dines with JG and Barrie at Romano's.
28 Goes to Brixton to see Catherine Willard in Ibsen's *Ghosts*.

December
3   (Mon) JC's sixtieth birthday. In London he continues to
    work on *AG* but also enjoys the social round with old
    friends – CG and Mrs Dummett, EG, the Colvins, W.L. George
    and others.
6   Dines at the RAC with JG, Barrie, Lucas and Gilbert
    Murray.
30 Writes to Gibbon that he has borrowed 'two Carlyles (of
    Froude) and two Goncourts'.

1918

January

1 (Tues) Despite lameness, JC works steadily on *AG*, with almost a quarter now written. He is encouraged by EG, who joins him at Hyde Park Mansions for the first night of the new year.

?18 Has been reading George Sand's *Histoire de ma vie* (1854–5); also borrows Vasari volumes from Colvin.

21 Colvin introduces a young admirer, Hugh Walpole, at the Carlton Hotel. Percy Anderson, also present, will paint JC's portrait later in the year. At the end of the month Walpole is invited to dine with the JCs and becomes a regular part of their circle.

31 JG visits and finds the Sandersons with JC.

February

1 (Fri) EG visits, followed by JG and the Sandersons in the coming week. Cecil Roberts meets JC at a *soirée* given by Lady Colefax this month and, on a later visit to see the writer, finds him with EG at work on *AG*.

6 Reads Ezra Pound's poetry, though with little sympathy.

The JCs' London stay comes to an end later in the month, when Jessie is well enough to make a trip to see John at his new school, Ripley Court.

March

4 (Mon) Completes 'Tradition' (*Daily Mail*, 6 Mar [*NLL*]), for which he receives 250 guineas from Northcliffe.

14 Becomes a member of the Athenaeum Club, nominated by Colvin and with the fee paid by Northcliffe.

24 Contact with Borys now restored after 10 days of worrying silence during an increased German offensive.

27 Reads the first of EG's war satires, later published as *Papa's War* (1919).

April

20 (Sat) Again afflicted by wartime gloom, JC prepares for a final effort on *AG*. Regular dictation of the novel from January onwards accounts for its remarkably speedy composition.

25 Meets Gosse at a preview of war pictures by WR at the Goupil Gallery, lunches with the artist, and is laid up on his return home.

May

1 (Wed) Thanks Gosse for a copy of *Father and Son* (1907), which he has already twice read.

14 The JCs see Congreve's *The Way of the World* performed by the English Stage Society in London.

17 Engaged in dictating the last chapter of *AG*, looks forward to a visit from Walpole.

26 JG at Capel House, finding JC very well. He is followed later in the month by Jean-Aubry.

June

2 (Sun) Walpole spends the weekend with JC, who is in fine form and gives his opinion on Walpole's *The Green Mirror* (1918).

4 Finishes *AG*, writing its First and Second Notes until the 14th. Soon after, the JCs leave for London, where Jessie requires further treatment on her leg.

24 Borys arrives in London on a fortnight's leave and joins the family, again at 4C Hyde Park Mansions. Soon after, Gide visits with some translated material for JC to see and approve.

26 Jessie enters the nursing home for her operation by Sir Robert Jones on the following day and will remain there six weeks. Both JC and Borys catch severe influenza, the latter having to postpone his return to France.

July

5 (Fri) Still in London, JC reads the manuscript of the unfinished *Rescue* in preparation for a decisive return to it in the autumn.

18 Borys is fit enough to return to France, though JC still feels thoroughly seedy.

August

10 (Sat) 'First News' appears in *Reveille* [*NLL*], edited by JG.

13 The JCs return from London, though Jessie has shown little improvement.

22 'Well Done!', written at the end of July to pay for current expenses, runs in the *Daily Chronicle* until the 24th [*NLL*].
24 *New Republic* (New York) prints 'Mr. Conrad is not a Jew', a letter from JC in response to a published jibe by Frank Harris.

September
7 (Sat) Still resting after finishing *AG*, JC enjoys being involved with the stage *Victory* and its casting.
16 Recent visitors include Dent and Walpole.
17 About this time the JCs learn that they will shortly have to move from Capel House.
25 Soon to escort Jessie to London for medical treatment, JC braces himself for a return to *The Rescue*.

October
1 (Tues) The JCs go to London for a fortnight, with JC staying at the Norfolk Hotel while Jessie is confined to hospital.
2 By this date JC breaks his agreement with Quinn by selling manuscripts to T.J. Wise, to whom he writes on the 10th, 'I am afraid Quinn will want to take my scalp when he hears of our transactions.'
9 In better health, JC returns to *The Rescue*, anticipating a January completion date and looking forward to his next project, *Suspense*.
10 Suffering from shell-shock, Borys has been admitted to hospital in Rouen.
c.24 *The Rescue* is now contracted for serialisation.

November
Much of the month is taken up with searching for a new house and several visits to Hartley Manor, Longfield (Kent), though this property is finally rejected.
11 (Mon) Armistice Day. JC's relief is mixed with apprehension that 'very blind forces are set free catastrophically all over the world' (to Walpole).
14 In London with Wladyslaw Sobański to see editors of *Land and Water* about a projected Polish article.
21 Completes part IV of *The Rescue*.
At the end of the month anticipates a visit by Siegfried Sassoon, whose poetry he reads in preparation for the meeting.

December

3   (Tues) JC's sixty-first birthday. Soon after, Borys begins a convalescence period at home. In the same month serialisation of *AG* begins in *Lloyd's Magazine* (until Feb 1920).

6   JC and JBP debate whether *The Rescue* should precede *AG* as a published volume.

14 House-hunting still preoccupies JC, though he is now at work on a Polish article.

18 Sees JBP in London.

27 Finishes 'The Crime of Partition' (*Fortnightly Review*, 1 May 1919 [*NLL*]).

1919

January

2   (Thurs) After a meeting today with Doubleday in London to discuss the forthcoming Collected Edition, JC is prevented from further work on *The Rescue* by a month's gout (coinciding with the death of the JCs' maid, Nellie Lyons, on the 20th). He looks forward to a visit from Walpole, whose *The Secret City* (1919) he has read.

29 Writes the Author's Note to *OI*.

30 Serialisation of *The Rescue* begins in *Land and Water*, continuing until 31 July.

February

6   (Thurs) The JCs go to London for further examinations on Jessie's leg, staying at Durrant's Hotel.

10 Meets EG. Two days later he visits the Surrey Scientific Company in Mortlake on Borys's behalf.

13 The JCs return home.

15 After his January illness JC resumes work on *The Rescue* (part V), hoping that it may help to win him the Nobel Prize.

19 Reads through his past correspondence to EG, which the latter plans to publish (and eventually does so in 1928).

21 Stephen Reynolds dies.

24 Looks forward to dramatising *SA*.

25 Sees Eric Pinker (EP) in London.

March

3 (Mon) Dines with Marie Löhr, producer of *Victory*. Has now started part VI of *The Rescue*.

25 The JCs take up temporary residence in Spring Grove, Wye, near Ashford (Kent).

26 First performance of *Victory* at the Globe Theatre, attended by Borys. JC possibly attends one of its 82 performances (it runs until 14 June).

April

12 (Sat) *AG* published by Doubleday, Page (by Unwin in Britain, 6 Aug), the first JC volume to have a first edition of more than 10,000 copies.

16 Finishes 'Confidence' (*Daily Mail*, 30 June [*NLL*]), after which he enters a three-week period of severe gout; Jessie is also painfully crippled.

May

9 (Fri) Recently cheered up by a long talk with JBP, he begins his final drive on *The Rescue*.

25 Finishes *The Rescue* 23 years after its first beginning, revising the last pages until the 28th.

June

7 (Sat) RC stays for the weekend when JC is again laid up with gout; he visits again on the 28th with Candler.

16 JBP sells the film rights of *Romance* for $5000, the sum shared equally between JC and FMF.

27 Thanks Colvin for a copy of Keats's *Letters*, having seen Colvin recently in London and stayed overnight with Gibbon.

July

11 (Fri) The JCs visit the Hopes in Colchester for the weekend, the first of several social occasions in July. They arrive home to greet Harriet Capes as a guest, followed by RC and the Wedgwoods later in the month.

August

2 (Sat) Gordon Gardiner arrives for the weekend, the first of many visitors this month, including EG (who stays for three days) and the JBPs.

6 Reads JG's *Another Sheaf* (1919).
7 Early notices of *AG* are 'very poor, puzzle-headed, hesitating pronouncements; yet not inimical' (to Colvin).
10 Walpole visits and finds JC in good form, though annoyed by reviews of *AG*. JC tells him that his favourite books to reread are Hudson's *Idle Days in Patagonia* (1893) and Alfred Wallace's *The Malay Archipelago* (1869).
20 JC is much impressed by Gide's *Journal sans dates* and now also reads W.L. George's *Blind Alley* (both 1919).
28 Again painfully crippled, Jessie is escorted to London for examinations on her leg and will require further operations.

September
2 (Tues) Dr Tebb has recently visited for two days, followed in mid-month by Frank Vernon and JBP, who come to discuss plans for dramatising *SA*.
21 JC's name appears with 200 others on a greetings message to Gosse on his seventieth birthday.
30 'Stephen Crane: A Note without Dates' finished by this date (*London Mercury*, Dec [*NLL*]).
During the summer JC writes four more Author's Notes (to *PR*, *TU*, *TOS* and *Mirror*) and, with EG's help, revises *The Rescue* for book publication.

October
2 (Thurs) Move begins from Spring Grove to Oswalds, Bishopsbourne, near Canterbury, JC's final home, with Grace Willard supervising its furnishing.
10 Leaves for a weekend with the JBPs at Burys Court. After his relaxed summer, he soon begins work on a four-act dramatisation of *SA*, with Act I 'nearly finished' by the 15th (to Colvin).
24 Sees JBP and Dent in London.

November
4 (Tues) JC's objection that the French translation of *AG* has been promised to a woman rather than Jean-Aubry leads to an awkward exchange with Gide.
9 Vernon visits to work on the dramatisation of *SA*; Act II finished the next day.

12 RC helps JC to compile items for inclusion in a planned volume of collected prose (*NLL*).
15 The JGs call to see Oswalds.
22 Fresh from reading CG's *Brought Forward* (1916), JC now finishes Act III of the play.
30 The JCs go to Liverpool (via London) for a month for Jessie's operation by Sir Robert Jones. In London for two days, JC sees Heinemann and confers with theatrical producers about his new play.

December
2 (Tues) On the day before JC's sixty-second birthday, Jessie undergoes her operation. She convalesces at the Sefton Nursing Home for most of the month.
While in Liverpool, JC gives his first formal public speech – on the traditions of the Merchant Marine – to the University Club, with David Bone there to give support. He also attends a lecture by Jean-Aubry, 'Verlaine et les musiciens'. Otherwise this month is unproductive, the later part spoilt by ill-health. The JCs arrive back at Oswalds before Christmas.

1920

January–February
Illness dominates the early part of the year when JC, on his return from Liverpool, is laid low for two months by influenza and then gout and depression. In bed much of the time, he slowly and painfully corrects proofs for the book edition of *The Rescue*, finishing on 24 February. Jessie develops shingles and, her recent operation having been unsuccessful, awaits further surgery. In the middle of these difficulties Karola Zagórska arrives (27 Feb) for a six-month stay. During the coming year JC is much concerned with plans for collections of his work, both collected editions and *NLL*.

March
3 (Wed) Completes Author's Note to *SA*.
15 The first draft of the stage *SA* is finished; it is revised over the next few days, then sent to Vernon and J.E. Vedrenne.

25 Receives a copy of RC's *Wanderings* (1920), already seen in manuscript.
26 RC visits while Jessie is laid up awaiting an operation on the 31st.

April

5 (Mon) Has read W.L. George's *Caliban* (1920).
6 The Polish–Soviet war begins, with the offensive in the Ukraine led by Pilsudski.
7 William Heinemann visits for lunch to discuss the forthcoming Collected Edition; JC is still afflicted by gout.
9 Finishes the Author's Note to *SS* and begins one to *TLS*.
10 Grants Aniela Zagórska the Polish translation rights to his works.
15 Has read CG's *A Brazilian Mystic* (1920).
19 Finishes reading the manuscript of JG's *In Chancery* (1920).
20 Jessie returns from the nursing home.
26 Sends a cablegram to the Committee for the Polish Government Loan, Washington, DC, in support of a Polish loan [*CDAUP*].

May

1 (Sat) Jessie undergoes another operation, this time at home.
6 In London to see JBP, JC returns to entertain RC at the weekend.
11 Has begun *Suspense* by this date. He will work on it intermittently right up to his death.
21 *The Rescue* published by Doubleday, Page (by Dent in Britain, 24 June), with JBP in attendance at Oswalds.
30 CG and Mrs Dummett make a Sunday visit.
During this month JC also writes Author's Notes to *UWE* and *Chance*, with those to *Victory* and *WT* already completed.

June

5 (Sat) Walpole visits for the weekend, hears JC's plans for *Suspense*, and meets RC.
7 JC travels with both men to London and does research at the British Museum. He is driven home by gout, which leaves him in 'the depth of dumps' for several days (to Walpole, 14 June).
23 He is back in London to see Dent.

July

2   (Fri) JC in London, bringing JBP back to Oswalds.
3   John Powell gives a weekend concert at Oswalds, playing *Rhapsodie Nègre* (based on 'Heart of Darkness') and Chopin; RC is also present before leaving for Burma.
18 On a weekend stay Walpole sees the opening section of *Suspense* and reports that JC said the FMF 'belittled everything he touched because he had a *small* soul' (Hart-Davis, *Hugh Walpole*, p. 195). CG and T.E. Lawrence visit for the day.
19 Northcliffe pays a visit.
21 In London to see JBP, returns home in readiness for another operation to Jessie's leg on the 24th.
24 In response to a request from Laurence Holt, director of a Liverpool shipping firm, JC has finished 'Memorandum on the Scheme for Fitting out a Sailing Ship' [*LE*].

August

The summer social round begins, with visits from JBP, Wise, Dent, Holt, the Hopes, and Ralph Pinker, who stays during Canterbury Cricket Week. A visit by the JCs to see Kipling at Bateman's, Burwash, probably takes place about this time. *Suspense* recedes into the background, only three chapters having been written by the 18th.

27 (Fri) In preparation for work on a film scenario, JC and JBP pay a visit to the 'moving pictures' at the Stoll, Kingsway, to see Hugo's *Les Misérables*.

September

1   (Wed) Having arrived at the Great Eastern Hotel in Deal the previous day, the JCs begin a three-week holiday (to the 21st) which provides JC with a mixture of pleasure – in the form of several boat-trips with John – and business. For the first fortnight he revises and arranges the contents of *NLL*.
13 JBP arrives. The two men begin a film scenario of 'Gaspar Ruiz', to be called *Gaspar the Strong Man*.

October

4   (Mon) EG arrives at Oswalds for a two-day visit.
5   Heinemann dies.
9   Finishes the Author's Note to *NLL*. Doubleday and his son

come for lunch; Walpole, whose *The Captives* (1920) JC has read, comes for the weekend.

12 Polish–Russian peace treaty signed.

29 By this date JC finishes the screenplay of *Gaspar the Strong Man*. He and JBP will later meet representatives of the Laski Film Company, though nothing comes of the cinema project.

31 JBP invited to Canterbury next week to see the recent Paramount film of *Victory*, the first film based on a JC novel.

November

JC's health and mood deteriorate during late autumn and leave him feeling 'gouty, seedy, crusty, moody . . . and lame' (to Harriet Capes, 17 Nov). Unfit for work on *Suspense*, he has been helping Jean-Aubry to translate the latter's 'Joseph Conrad's Confessions' into English.

18 (Thurs) Interviewed by Ernest Rhys for an article in *The Bookman* (New York); on arrival Rhys finds him reading an Edith Wharton novel.

22 Jessie goes to London for a week, where JC joins her on the 25th and lunches with Dr Mackintosh at Brown's Hotel to discuss plans for Borys's new job with the Surrey Scientific Company in Mortlake. JC then proceeds to Burys Court for a weekend with the JBPs.

December

3 (Fri) JC's sixty-third birthday.

4 Mackintosh is invited to Oswalds to meet JBP on a weekend visit.

10 Finishes a draft of *Laughing Anne* (a two-act dramatisation of 'Because of the Dollars'), which he revises and expands over the following week.

17 A busy JC settles his affairs in London prior to a forthcoming visit to Corsica, the first batch of *NLL* proofs having arrived the day before.

20 S.A. Everitt visits, followed soon after by a group of Polish guests including the composer Karol Szymanowski.

23 Has read CG's *Cartagena and the Banks of the Sinú* (1920).

25 Visitors during the Christmas season include Jean-Aubry and Catherine Willard.

1921

January

5 (Wed) In London to see Pawling about a missing dedication in a volume of the Heinemann Collected Edition, which begins to appear this month.

12 Attends a gathering at Brown's Hotel with EG, JBP and Jean-Aubry. Jean-Aubry soon pays a visit, as does Walpole to persuade JC to write a foreword to *A Hugh Walpole Anthology* (1921).

23 The JCs depart for a three-month stay on Corsica, where Jessie will convalesce and JC endeavour to resume work on *Suspense*. Borys drives them, via the battlefields at Armentières, as far as Rouen.

25 They leave Rouen on their way south; Jean-Aubry will accompany them as far as Lyon.

30 In Marseille for about three days, where JC visits old haunts and from where they sail to Corsica.

February

3 (Thurs) By this date they settle in at the Grand Hôtel d'Ajaccio, soon joined by the JBPs. They meet Alice Kinkead and H.-R. Lenormand, who lends JC two of Freud's works, which are returned unread.

11 Visit to Napoleon's house.

24 Miss Hallowes arrives to be on hand for work on *Suspense*.

26 Borrows numerous books on Napoleon from the town library, including Stendhal's *Vie de Napoléon* (1876).

25 *NLL* published by Dent (in America by Doubleday, Page, 22 Apr), later attracting reviews by E.M. Forster and Virginia Woolf.

March

17 (Thurs) Reports that he has been unable to do much serious work: 'Head empty. Feelings as one dead' (to EG). Finishes the promised foreword for Walpole's anthology [*CDAUP*].

24 The JCs' silver wedding anniversary.

This spring or late the preceding winter JC apparently meets Chodźko in Toulon (a special trip from Corsica?), then (or in Apr) is taken to Giens Peninsula by Mme Alvar to refresh his recollections of the area for *The Rover*.

April

7   (Thurs) They leave Corsica.

10 After travelling back via Nice and Toulon, they arrive home to find that the Mortlake company has collapsed and Borys is unemployed.

Late this month JC sees Norman McKinnel to find out his plans for the stage *SA* and also meets the JGs.

May

10 (Tues) Despite his researches on Corsica and optimism to JBP, JC has made little progress with *Suspense* and informs JG, 'I can't get my teeth into the novel.'

June

1   (Wed) Alice Kinkead arrives for a week's stay, followed by Walpole, then JBP, and later the Colvins for a weekend.

12 Acknowledges receipt of Bruno Winawer's Polish play *Księga Hioba* (*The Book of Job*), which he has probably already started to translate himself and will finish on the 25th.

17 RC comes for the weekend on his return from the East.

27 Sees JG's *The Family Man* at the Comedy Theatre and there passes on *The Book of Job* to McKinnel.

July

27 (Wed) 'The Dover Patrol' appears in *The Times* [*LE*]. JC picks up John from his Tonbridge school, then goes to Burys Court, and returns two days later in JBP's splendid coach-and-four.

The JBPs stay until 8 August and attend various events at the Canterbury Cricket Festival. The happy social mood is temporarily broken in late July by an angry exchange of letters with Mackintosh about the failure of the Mortlake company and collapse of Borys's prospects.

August–September

Late summer brings further visits and visitors – Elbridge Adams, RC, JBP, S.A. Everitt and the Hopes. In response to EG (who has been reading the *Suspense* manuscript), JC is unable to recommend Stefan Zeromski's *The History of a Sin* – which he first read much earlier – for translation, on the grounds that it is 'gratuitously ferocious' (to EG, 2 Sep). He responds more favourably to his other reading of the time, Winawer's *Groteski* (1921). At the end

of September, JC succumbs to painful gout, which continues into
October.

October
8   (Sat) Walpole spends an uncomfortable weekend with JC, who
    still suffers from gout; Sydney Cockerell is also present.
9   Completes a short preface [*CDAUP*] to Kinkead's *Landscapes
    of Corsica and Ireland* (1921). Ready to lay *Suspense* aside, JC
    begins a short story (destined to become *The Rover*), though
    he makes little progress with it until December.
15 RC arrives for a weekend visit.
17 By this date completes 'The Loss of the *Dalgonar'* (*London
    Mercury*, Dec [*LE*]).
c.21 Russell and his wife visit, followed later in the month by the
    Grant Watsons.
29 At Burys Court for the weekend with JBP, meets American
    film-producers to discuss *Gaspar the Strong Man*.

November
1   (Tues) Suffering from the after-effects of gout, JC has read JG's
    To Let (1921), the last Forsyte volume, and Colvin's *Memories
    and Notes* (1921).
3   Spends the night in London (where Jessie is staying) and
    lunches with Doubleday the next day.
18 Has recently read Russell's *The Analysis of Mind* (1921) and
    enjoys a Berenson study of Italian Renaissance painters.
26 RC and Gardiner stay for the weekend.
30 Has been reading FWD's *The Gift of Paul Clermont* (1921).

December
3   (Sat) JC's sixty-fourth birthday.
6   Approached by FMF to settle old debts, he sends £20.
    Complains to CG of the persistent depression that follows
    upon 'the inability to work seriously'.
9   By this date has begun *The Rover* in earnest, with *Suspense*
    laid aside for a year.
21 JC's response to a questionnaire on 'The First Thing I
    Remember' appears in *John O'London's Weekly* [*CDAUP*].
24 RC arrives to spend Christmas at Oswalds.
30 Visits JBP in London and then accompanies him to Burys
    Court.

In this year *The Secret Agent. Drama in Four Acts* is privately printed for the author by H.J. Goulden. Of 1921 JC will soon say, 'I could not work properly . . . I could not even concentrate my thoughts without a great effort. This makes me worried and fretful' (to Aniela Zagórska, 27 Jan 1922).

1922

January
After his return from Burys Court and a visit from Jean-Aubry, JC is laid low with influenza and gout for virtually the whole of January.
27 (Fri) Reads Constance Garnett's translation of Chekhov's plays (1922).
28 JBP leaves for America, taking the unfinished *Suspense* with him.

February
8   (Wed) JBP dies suddenly in New York. JC's affairs are now taken over by Eric Pinker (EP), who visits soon after.
9   Still unwell, JC complains, 'I have done no work to speak of for months' (to Ada Galsworthy).
23 Accompanies Jessie to London for an examination on her leg.

March
11 (Sat) RC and EP make a weekend visit, both again seeing JC in London on the 23rd.
27 Reads Jean-Aubry's *La Musique et les nations* (1922).

April
9   (Sun) JC in bed with gout, where he has been for four days. Further illness later in the month holds up progress on *The Rover*, though he is able to advise RC about his article 'Joseph Conrad and the East'.

May
Now recovered, JC works purposefully on *The Rover*, writing 10 chapters in May and June.
6   (Sat) RC invited for a weekend visit.
11 Meets RC at the RAC and then sees EP, with whom he stays overnight at Burys Court.

19 Declines offer of an honorary degree from Oxford University.
24 Has read EG's *Friday Nights* (1922).
25 RC expected for the weekend.

June
20 (Tues) Jean-Aubry pays a visit.
27 Finishes *The Rover*, revising and expanding until 16 July.
    Meets EP in London on the 30th.

July
 2 (Sun) CG and Mrs Dummett pay a visit. Has read CG's
    The Conquest of New Granada (1922).
 4 The JCs in London for the coming week, staying at the
    Curzon Hotel.
 7 First contact with Walter Tittle. This week (at a party given
    by Lady Colefax) JC meets Valéry and Ravel, the latter also
    playing for him at the home of Mme Alvar.
 9 Lunches with CG at Claridge's to discuss a solution to
    the heavy debts recently incurred by Borys.
22 Borys visits for the weekend, looking forward to his new
    job with Daimler in mid-August.
25 Sits for a portrait by Tittle.

August
 1 (Tues) Finishes preface to RC's *Into the East* (1923), later
    titled 'Travel' [*LE*].
 7 Browses through the new collected edition of JG's *The
    Forsyte Saga* (1922).
 8 Draws up his will, with RC and Ralph Wedgwood as
    executors.
14 Northcliffe dies.
18 Hudson dies.
22 In London on business, and again later in the month for
    meetings with JG and EG.

September
 2 (Sat) Borys is married, though the news is kept from his
    father for nine months.
12 JC contemplates Sybil Thorndike for the role of Mrs Verloc
    in the stage *SA*.
14 The JCs leave for Liverpool, from where, as guests of Sir

Robert Jones, they take a three-day tour of North Wales, returning to London on the 19th. After his long summer break, JC now resolves to return to *Suspense*.

October

In a busy month dominated by the forthcoming stage production of *SA*, JC is frequently in London, having discussions with its producer, Harry Benrimo, and attending rehearsals of the play. He also meets several friends – Garland on the 4th, the now invalid Hope (11th), Tittle (23rd), Valéry, Ravel and the ever-present RC. In between trips he manages to read David Garnett's *Lady into Fox* (1922) and corresponds with Russell about the latter's *Problems of China* (1922).

November

1   (Wed) At the dress rehearsal of *SA*.
2   When the play opens at the Ambassadors Theatre, he chooses not to attend, being interviewed by R.L. Mégroz at the Curzon.
3   Makes cuts to the play after its unfavourable reception. The next day Jessie goes to witness their effect.
11 The play is taken off after 10 performances. Finishes 'Outside Literature' (*Manchester Guardian*, 4 Dec [*LE*]).
12 Tittle, Allan Wade and his wife pay a Sunday visit.
18 The JCs give hospitality to Sir Maurice Cameron and his wife, driving them around Surrey in search of rooms for Alice Kinkead.
21 Has been reading 'nothing but Marcel Proust' (to Sandeman) and three days later comments on Zofia Kossak-Szczucka's *Pozoga* (1923).
27 In London to see EP, JC also attends a Hudson memorial meeting at Dent's office, where he meets J.C. Squire and Rhys.

December

3   (Sun) JC's sixty-fifth birthday.
6   In London, meets RC at the RAC and then lunches with Doubleday, who presses him to visit America next spring.
14 Having returned to *Suspense*, JC now decides upon its publication title.
23 Pawling dies.

25   Christmas at home, with RC in attendance and Borys making a New Year's Eve visit.
30   Plays with the idea of living in France to reduce income tax. Acknowledges the first Polish translation of *AF* (by Aniela Zagórska), a copy of which he sends to EG. JC's reading at this time includes Laforgue's poetry.

1923

January–February
The month opens with a visit from C.K. Scott-Moncrieff (translator of Proust), whose *Marcel Proust, an English Tribute* (1923) includes extracts from JC's letter on 'Proust as Creator' [*CDAUP*]. Then JC applies himself to serious work on *Suspense*, reaching the end of part III by the beginning of March. By mid-February he has virtually decided to make the trip to America and asks RC to accompany him (the latter declines). JC's reading includes Tadeusz Żuk-Skarszewski's *Rumak Swiatowida* (1919) and Valéry's poetry.

March
7   (Wed) Has read Ernst Bendz's *Joseph Conrad* and writes to the author.
8   Knopf and Thomas Beer visit, persuading JC to contribute a preface to Beer's *Stephen Crane* (1923).
12   After a weekend entertaining Gardiner, begins the Crane preface and finishes it on the 23rd [*LE*].
15   Declines an honorary degree from Cambridge University, having already refused such offers from several other universities.
29   By this date finishes 'His War Book' [*LE*], preface to a new edition of Crane's *The Red Badge of Courage* (1925).
30   Jacob Epstein visits.

April
8   (Sun) Borys visits before his father's departure for America.
16   JC leaves home for his forthcoming trip and calls on the Hopes in Colchester, dining with RC at the Curzon in the evening.
17   Gives a speech to the Lifeboat Institution at the Aeolian

Hall in the afternoon [*CDAUP*]; attends a *soirée* at the home
of Mme Alvar, where guests include Bennett and Ravel.
18 Bids farewell to friends in London for the next two days,
with Jessie arriving in town on the 19th.
20 Goes to Glasgow, accompanied by RC. Dines with admirers,
including Neil Munro.
21 Sails from Glasgow for America in the *Tuscania*, commanded
by an old friend, David Bone, whose brother Muirhead also
makes the trip to entertain and draw JC. During the voyage
writes 'Ocean Travel' (London *Evening News*, 15 May [*LE*]).

May
Arriving in New York on the 1st to a noisy and boisterous
welcome, JC goes to stay with the Doubledays at Effendi Hill,
Oyster Bay, NY. In the coming month he is fêted in princely
fashion and lionised by old friends, distant admirers, celebrated
Americans and Poles (including Paderewski). Doubleday organises press interviews and sittings for a portrait by Oscar Cesare.
Published this month, A.J. Dawson's *Britain's Life-Boats* includes
a foreword by JC [*CDAUP*].
3 (Thurs) Piano recital by Powell at Effendi Hill.
5 Addresses 'fellow' employees at Doubleday, Page in Garden
City, NY.
7 Interviewed by a large group of American journalists.
10 Reads from *Victory* at the home of Mrs Curtiss James to
an audience of 200.
15 Leaves for a motor-tour of New England and Boston with
the Doubledays. His tour takes him to Yale and Harvard universities, the houses of Longfellow and Lowell, and Boston
harbour.
22 The party stays overnight with Adams, returning to Effendi
Hill on the 24th, where JC relaxes until his departure.

June
2 (Sat) Sails from New York in the *Majestic* with the Doubledays.
9 Arrives in Southampton and travels to the Norfolk Hotel to
be met by news that Borys has been secretly married since
last September. Distressed and shaken, JC spends much of
June sorting out his feelings about the affair, paying for his
exertions with an attack of gout later.
11 Eager to avoid a direct break with his son, JC arranges for

an allowance to be paid to Borys. 'Marrying is not a crime'
(to EP).

12 The Doubledays are entertained at Oswalds.
21 JC has written to Borys telling him to regard the allowance
    as a wedding present.

July
3 (Tues) Finishes 'Christmas Day at Sea' (*Daily Mail*, 24 Dec
   [*LE*]).
9 Resumes work on *Suspense*.
13 In London to lunch with Page and EP.
15 Borys and his wife pay their first visit to Oswalds.
18 Page and his wife visit.
30 RC leaves after a weekend stay, followed by Borys and
   his wife on this and the following weekend.

August
5 (Sun) Visit by Hamlin Garland, followed later in the month
   by the Clifford family.
29 Finishes 'The *Torrens*: A Personal Tribute' (*Blue Peter*, Oct
   [*LE*]).

September
3 (Mon) In London to meet EP and RC.
9 The JCs go to the Curzon Hotel prior to leaving for France.
11 They travel to Le Havre to see the home of Pastor Charles
   Bost, where John will lodge in order to improve his French.
   They call on Jean-Aubry's parents, and JC goes to see Gide
   in Cuverville only to find that he is not at home.
16 On arrival at Oswalds, JC retires to bed with a temperature
   for four days.
23 Has recently read JG's *Captures* (1923).
26 The JCs migrate to the Curzon Hotel for three days while
   water-pipes are repaired at Oswalds.
Serialisation of *The Rover* begins this month in the *Pictorial
Review* (New York).

October
20 (Sat) Despite some illness in the month, JC manages a
   social weekend, with RC, Jean-Aubry, Walpole, Muirhead
   Bone and Valéry in attendance.

November

8 (Thurs) FMF writes to propose republication of *The Nature of a Crime*.

12 Despite persistent illness, JC manages to finish 'Geography and Some Explorers' (*Countries of the World*, Feb 1924 [*LE*]). Auction of Quinn's Conradiana begins in New York.

19 Borys visits, asking his father for a loan of £75.

30 Illness keeps JC in bed, where he enjoys EG's edition of *Letters from W.H. Hudson* (1923).

December

1 (Sat) Publication of *The Rover* by Doubleday, Page (by Unwin in Britain, 3 Dec), its serialisation finishing this month.

3 JC's sixty-sixth birthday.

10 Laid up with gout for the next few days, he is visited by EP on the 12th.

Christmas finds the JCs unwell, though they entertain a small party, including Jean-Aubry, and Gertrude and Muirhead Bone.

1924

January

2 (Wed) Still an invalid and now entering the last year of his life, JC finishes reading Bennett's *Riceyman Steps* (1923).

6 First of several sittings this month for a portrait by Tittle (now in the National Portrait Gallery).

11 The JCs' first grandson, Philip James Conrad, born.

16 They go to London to see the new baby. Jessie's knee is examined the next morning, after which JC lunches with RC, who visits Oswalds later in the month.

29 Grudgingly agrees to republication of *The Nature of a Crime* in *Transatlantic Review*.

February

1 (Fri) Still at work on *Suspense*.

2 Borys and wife bring their new baby to Oswalds.

4 FMF pays a visit – a suspicious JC finds him 'too friendly' (to EP, 7 Feb). They negotiate their collaborative properties, and FMF persuades JC to write a preface to *The Nature of a Crime*.

6   JC in London to see EP.
27 The JCs visit Sir Robert Jones in London.

March
Most of the month is given over to the sculptor Epstein, but JC is
unable to stand the strain and Epstein has to return home before
the bust (now in the National Portrait Gallery) is finished. Epstein
later recalled, 'He was crippled with rheumatism, crotchety,
nervous, and ill. He said to me, "I am finished"' (*Epstein: An
Autobiography*, p. 74).

April
25 (or 2 May) (Fri) Clifford comes for a weekend visit. About
    this time JC reads JG's *The Forest* (1924).
30 FMF turns up unexpectedly to see JC for the last time.

May
 3 (Sat) RC visits for lunch.
 5 JC finishes preface to *The Shorter Tales of Joseph Conrad* [LE].
11 Reads David Garnett's *The Man in the Zoo* (1924).
14 Finishes preface to *The Nature of a Crime* (*Transatlantic
    Review*, July [CDAUP]) and sends it to FMF on the 17th.
27 Declines Ramsay MacDonald's offer of a knighthood.
31 Has read presentation copy of Francis McCullagh's *The
    Bolshevik Persecution of Christianity* (1924).

June
11 (Wed) In London for lunch at the Polish Legation.
13 Knee operation for Jessie by Sir Robert Jones, with Borys
    and John visiting.
Others visitors this month include Jean-Aubry and Irena
Rakowska, a distant relative of JC's.

July
 4 (Fri) While Jessie recuperates in a nursing home, RC visits to
    cheer up a depressed JC; CG also visits on Sunday.
 8 At work on 'Legends', unfinished at his death (*Daily Mail*,
    15 Aug [LE]), but feeling 'languid and depressed' (to EP).
24 Jessie arrives home after convalescence.
26 Visits from Irena Rakowska and Grace Willard at this time.

August

1 (Fri) RC arrives for his last weekend with JC.

2 Seized with chest pains during a car-ride in the morning, JC is attended by doctors; Borys, his wife and son arrive with John later in the day, when JC complains of breathing difficulties.

3 Dies of a heart attack at 8.30 a.m.

7 Funeral service at St Thomas's Roman Catholic Church, Canterbury. Mourners include EG, RC, CG, Hugh Dent, Jean-Aubry, Meldrum, the Wedgwoods, Wise, Gardiner, Retinger and Cockerell. 'To those who attended Conrad's funeral in Canterbury during the Cricket Festival of 1924, and drove through the crowded streets festooned with flags, there was something symbolical of England's hospitality and in the crowd's ignorance of even the existence of this great writer. A few old friends, acquaintances and pressmen stood by his grave', writes EG (*Letters from John Galsworthy, 1900–1932*, ed. Edward Garnett, 1934, pp. 14–15).

September

26 (Fri) *The Nature of a Crime* published by Duckworth (in America by Doubleday, Page simultaneously).

October

5 (Sun) FMF completes *Joseph Conrad: A Personal Remembrance* in Bruges, published in November.

21 *Laughing Anne, and One Day More* published by Castle (by Doubleday, Page in America, 8 May 1925).

November

17 (Mon) *The Times* reports the gross value of JC's estate at his death as £20,045.

December

4 (Thurs) Jessie attacks FMF's memoir in *The Times Literary Supplement*.

In the years immediately following JC's death and prior to 1930, a number of unpublished writings were printed and scattered items collected, notable collections being *TH*, introduced by

CG (1925), and *LE* (1926). The novel unfinished at his death, *Suspense*, began serialisation in the *Saturday Review of Literature* (New York) on 27 June 1925 and ended on 12 September, just a few days before publication in book form. Numerous volumes of letters and memoirs soon followed, with Jean-Aubry already planning his two-volume *Life and Letters* in 1925 and publishing it in 1927. In the next three years further important collections of correspondence appeared – by Jessie (1927), RC (1928), EG (1928) and Jean-Aubry (1930). Of the memoirs published during the 1920s *Joseph Conrad as I Knew Him* (1926) by Jessie, who outlived her husband by 12 years, purports to be the most 'intimate', though many of JC's friends believed at the time that it renders him an injustice. The other important memoir is by JC's Boswell-figure, RC, who paid his homage in *The Last Twelve Years of Joseph Conrad* (1928).

Select Who's Who

Anderson, Jane (born 1893), an attractive Georgia-born journalist and wife of the composer Deems Taylor, was introduced to the Conrads in April 1916. Her animated contacts with the family during that year produced contrasting reactions. While Conrad relished her presence and pronounced her 'yum-yum' (to RC, 20 Aug 1916), Jessie came to feel that 'our fair American friend had been amusing herself at my expense' (JCC, p. 207). In Paris in 1917, Borys was smitten by the charms of 'the American flying girl', as was Retinger in a more serious way.

Barrie, James Matthew (1860–1937; knighted 1913), the Scottish novelist and dramatist, seems to have entered Conrad's sphere in 1903 with moral and considerable financial support, though their subsequent relationship was probably not close. In 1904 Conrad sent his first dramatic adaptation, *One Day More*, for a reading by the dramatist who had just enjoyed a *succès d'estime* with *Peter Pan*.

Bennett, Enoch Arnold (1867–1931), the chronicler of Potteries life in such works as *The Old Wives' Tale* (1908) and *The Clayhanger Trilogy* (1910–15), was – with Wells and Garnett – an early admirer and champion of Conrad's fiction, which he regularly reviewed as assistant editor of *Academy* in the late 1890s. Introduced to each other by Wells in 1901, their paths crossed only infrequently in later years, though Bennett remained an appreciative and discriminating reader of Conrad's work. For his part, Conrad read some of Bennett's novels and corresponded with him on the virtues and vices of the naturalistic method. See also Owen Knowles, 'Arnold Bennett as an "Anonymous" Reviewer of Conrad's Early Fiction', *The Conradian*, x (1985) 26–36.

Blackwood, William (1836–1912), grandson of the original publisher and founder of the Edinburgh *Blackwood's Magazine*, published Conrad's works between 1897 and 1902. Conrad also knew his two nephews, George (1876–1942) and James (1878–1951).

Bobrowska, Teofila (died 1875), wife of Józef Bobrowski (1790–1850) and Conrad's maternal grandmother, was appointed guardian to her beloved 'Konradek' in 1870 after his parents' death.

Bobrowski, Tadeusz (1829–94), Conrad's maternal uncle and self-appointed guardian from 1869, read law at St Petersburg University before becoming head of the Bobrowski family in 1859. His memoirs (published in 1900, republished in 1979, and extracted in *CUFE*) tend to confirm Conrad's later impression of his uncle as 'a man of powerful intelligence and great force of character' (to EG, 20 Jan 1900). Bobrowski regarded himself as continuing the enlightened liberal traditions of his family and prided himself on his clear-headed prudence and consistency of purpose, in contrast to what he saw as the impulsive and foolhardy idealism of the Korzeniowskis. As Conrad's guardian, Bobrowski granted his nephew permission to leave Poland for Marseille in 1874, overseeing his career and finances for the next 15 years. Conrad's letters to his uncle were destroyed during the 1917 October Revolution. Bobrowski's letters, together with the 'Document' he compiled on Conrad's early life and background (see Najder, *Conrad's Polish Background*, pp. 183–202), show the seriousness with which he took his guardianship and invariably find him pressing the gospel of work and stabilising commitment upon a young man in whom he detected strains of 'Korzeniowski' impulsiveness. A year after Bobrowski's death Conrad dedicated his first novel, *Almayer's Folly*, to the uncle 'to whom I stand more in the relation of a son than a nephew' (to EG, 20 Jan 1900).

Bone, David William (1874–1959; knighted 1946), one of three talented brothers of a Clydeside family, was a seaman-author who corresponded with Conrad in 1910. In 1923 Bone, then a senior commander with the Anchor Line, captained the *Tuscania*, in which Conrad sailed to America, a voyage remembered in Bone's *Landfall at Sunset: The Life of a Contented Sailor* (1955). His brother Muirhead (1876–1953; knighted 1937), a talented artist, also made the trip and became a friend of the Conrads. James Bone (1872–1962) was London editor of the *Manchester Guardian*.

Capes, Harriet Mary (1849–1936), writer of uplifting literature for children and sister of the novelist Bernard Capes, was a friend of the Conrads from 1895 and later compiled *Wisdom and Beauty from Conrad* (1915). Conrad dedicated *A Set of Six* to her.

Casement, Roger David (1864–1916; knighted 1911), British consular official and Irish nationalist, travelled and worked widely in Africa, where he first met Conrad in 1890. Their next significant contact occurred in 1903 when Casement, then in the consular service, prepared a government report on atrocities in Leopold's Congo and tried to interest Conrad in the newly established Congo Reform Association. After a distinguished diplomatic career, Casement's involvement with the Irish National Volunteers and collusion with Germany during the war led to his arrest for treason and execution in 1916. In that year Conrad described Casement as a 'truly tragic personality' (to Quinn, 24 May), though he declined to add his name to a plea for clemency.

Chesson, Wilfrid Hugh (1870–1952), an employee of T. Fisher Unwin, was probably the first professional reader to see the manuscript of *Almayer's Folly* and spot its promise.

Clifford, Hugh Charles (1866–1941; knighted 1909), combined a distinguished career as a colonial administrator and governor (in Malaya, North Borneo, Trinidad and Tobago, Africa and Ceylon) with that of a man of letters. An early admirer of Conrad, whose Eastern world naturally attracted him, he wrote one of the first general appreciations of Conrad's work. Conrad's review of Clifford's *Studies in Brown Humanity* (1898) led to a meeting in 1899, when both were fellow contributors to *Blackwood's*. Thereafter they corresponded, exchanged volumes, and entered into discussion of each other's work. Clifford continued to champion his friend's reputation, though his assertion (in *North American Review*, 1904) that Conrad at the beginning of his writing career wavered between French and English always irritated the writer. Conrad dedicated *Chance* (1914) to Clifford in acknowledgement of his help in securing an invitation to contribute a serial to the *New York Herald* (where *Chance* first appeared).

Colvin, Sidney (1845–1927; knighted 1911), a cultured critic of the fine arts and literature, was a friend and admirer of both Conrad and Stevenson (whose letters and works he edited). After a period as Slade Professor of Fine Art at Cambridge, he became Keeper in the Department of Prints and Drawings at the British Museum. He and his wife Frances maintained regular social contact with the Conrads from 1905 onwards. See also E.V. Lucas, *The Colvins and their Friends* (1928).

Conrad, Jessie Emmeline, *née* **George** (1873–1936), was one of nine children in a lower middle-class family which had been left in straitened circumstances in 1893 by the death of the father, variously described as 'warehouseman' and 'bookseller'. According to Conrad, he and Jessie (16 years his junior) first made serious contact in late 1894, when she was a typist in the City living with her widowed mother in Peckham. After a sudden proposal of marriage they were married on 24 March 1896 at Hanover Square registry office. In a letter of that time Conrad described his prospective bride as 'a small, not at all striking-looking person (to tell the truth alas – rather plain!) who is nevertheless very dear to me' (to Zagórski, 10 Mar 1896). Later impressions of Jessie by Conrad's friends (and biographers) are variable and sometimes unflattering, though Borys has suggested that her 'rigid self-control' and imperviousness to her husband's volatile moods made her 'the ideal wife for Joseph Conrad' (*MFJC*, p. 12). Conrad dedicated the *Youth* volume and *Romance* (with Elsie Hueffer) to her. A dislocated knee during childhood left Jessie prone to severe leg trouble and, after a fall in 1904, she was virtually permanently disabled. She ventured into print with *A Handbook of Cookery for a Small House* (completed 1907, published 1923, with a foreword by Conrad) and after Conrad's death published two intimate but often unreliable memoirs, *Joseph Conrad as I Knew Him* (1926) and *Joseph Conrad and his Circle* (1935). Their two sons extended the collection of family memoirs with *My Father: Joseph Conrad* (1970) by Borys (1898–1978), and *Joseph Conrad: Times Remembered* (1981) by John (1906–1982). To the first of his sons Conrad dedicated *The Shadow-Line* and *The Inheritors* (with Christina Hueffer).

Crane, Stephen (1871–1900), the brilliant young American writer and journalist, was introduced to Conrad by Pawling in 1897 some months after Crane's arrival in England. Before their meeting Conrad had already read *The Red Badge of Courage* (1895) and admired its experimental 'impressionist' methods, while Crane was an early admirer of *The Nigger of the 'Narcissus'*, which he read in proof. The two men were soon sufficiently confident of their friendship to contemplate a collaboration (on a play to be called 'The Predecessor'), though the project did not materialise. Their friendship was interrupted in 1898 by Crane's departure for the Spanish-American War as a correspondent and cut short by his early death in 1900. Conrad later wrote three appreciations of Crane and his work, one collected in *Notes on Life and Letters* and two in *Last Essays*.

Curle, Richard Henry Parnell (1883–1968), 25 years Conrad's junior, first met the writer in 1912 after having written about him in the *Manchester Guardian* and *Rhythm*. Their friendship proved to be lasting, with Curle filling the gap left by Ford. He became a regular part of the Conrad household and fulfilled the functions of a devoted Boswell. In between his duties as a newspaper editor and journalist (both at home with the *Daily Mail* and abroad) Curle wrote extensively about Conrad. His *Joseph Conrad: A Study* (1914), written with the author's approval and help, was the first full-length book on Conrad's fiction. This was followed after Conrad's death by *The Last Twelve Years of Joseph Conrad* (1928), an edition of Conrad's letters to Curle (1928), and *Joseph Conrad and his Characters* (1957). While making use of Curle's links with the press and basking in the younger man's adulatory respect, Conrad also enjoyed Curle's company and valued the sound practical sense of the friend to whom he dedicated *The Arrow of Gold*. At Oswalds when the novelist died, Curle was a co-executor of Conrad's will.

Dawson, Alec John (1872–1951) and his brother Ernest (died 1960), lived in Rye and 'were very real friends of the family' (John Conrad, *Joseph Conrad: Times Remembered*, p. 76). Both were writers and in connection with their army duties had travelled in India and the East, a common source of interest between them and Conrad.

Dawson, Francis Warrington (1878–1962), the son of a wealthy newspaper-owner from Charleston, South Carolina, was a successful international journalist and aspiring novelist when he arranged an introduction to Conrad in May 1910. Then recovering from a breakdown, Conrad responded to the polished charm of his young American admirer, who lived in France and much enjoyed the company of the celebrated. Conrad subsequently read Dawson's manuscripts and helped to revise and promote his work, though he resisted his invitation to join the Fresh Air Art Society. The relationship was at its most intimate during 1913–14, after which Dawson became an invalid and was unable to leave his home in Versailles.

Doubleday, Frank Nelson (1862–1934), American publisher, was responsible for the first American edition of *Lord Jim* (in partnership with McClure) and, with Heinemann, helped to subsidise Conrad during his early trials with *The Rescue*. In 1913, as chairman of his own company (Doubleday, Page), he took over as Conrad's main American publisher and, from the publication of *Chance* (1913) onwards, played a major role in shaping Conrad's American reputation. He campaigned to popularise the author in America, acquired American rights to his novels for a collected edition, and arranged Conrad's visit to America in 1923, when the author stayed at 'Effendi's' Long Island home.

Douglas, (George) Norman (1868–1952), polymath, epicurean and author of *South Wind* (1917). Of Scottish descent, he was the product of a cosmopolitan culture – brought up in Austria and Germany, widely travelled in the diplomatic service, and later resident in Italy. He met Conrad on Capri in 1905 when Douglas had only published anonymously. Conrad went on to recommend his writings to British publishers and established contacts for him with the *English Review*, of which he became assistant editor (1912–15). Conrad's services to the restless and unconventional Douglas included giving a home to his son Robin during school vacations. In 1915 Douglas's increasingly unhampered homosexual adventurism and subsequent arrest made it necessary for him to leave Britain. See also Frederick R. Karl, 'Joseph Conrad, Norman Douglas, and the *English Review*', *Journal of Modern Literature*, II (1971–2) 342–56; and Mark Holloway, *Norman Douglas: A Biography* (1976).

Epstein, Jacob (1880–1959), sculptor, undertook his famous bust of Conrad (now at the National Portrait Gallery) in the last year of the author's life. Epstein's recollection of their conversations in March 1924 can be found in *Let There Be Sculpture: An Autobiography* (1940) and *Epstein: An Autobiography* (1955).

Ford, Ford Madox (1873–1939), of Anglo-German parentage and brought up in Pre-Raphaelite circles, changed his surname from Hueffer in 1919. Later an important novelist and critic in his own right, Ford had published little when he first met Conrad in 1898. Soon after, the two committed themselves to a working collaboration which yielded *The Inheritors* (1901), *Romance* (1903) and *The Nature of a Crime* (written 1906). None of these brought the artistic success, recognition and financial reward anticipated by the two writers. During their 10-year friendship, significantly coinciding with Conrad's major period as a writer, 'there was, beneath Conrad's fierce pride, a real dependence on Ford. It was never a dependence for a knowledge of his craft or for imaginative insight . . . It was psychological support – assurance that these gifts were really his – that Conrad needed, and for it he expressed extravagant gratitude' (Mizener, *The Saddest Story: A Biography of Ford Madox Ford*, p. 46). In addition, there is no reason to doubt Ford's claim that at the height of their friendship he was heavily involved in Conrad's 'literary dustings and sweepings, correcting his proofs, writing from his dictation, suggesting words when he was at a loss, or bringing to his memory incidents that he had forgotten' (*Thus to Revisit*, 1921, p. 191). Their friendship foundered in 1909, partly through Conrad's disapproval of the distress caused by Ford's chaotic private life, but also through the latter's inability to manage the *English Review*, which he founded and edited. After the First World War, in which he was gassed, Ford lived more or less permanently in France and America, and his works of this time include *The Good Soldier* (1915) and *Parade's End* (1923–8). Later Ford wrote repeatedly and at length – but most memorably in *Joseph Conrad: A Personal Remembrance* (1924) – on his collaboration with Conrad, their shared love of French literary traditions, and plans for the 'new novel'. In addition to Mizener's biography, see Douglas Goldring, *The Last Pre-Raphaelite* (1948), and Raymond T. Brebach, *Joseph Conrad, Ford Madox Ford and the Making of 'Romance'* (Ann Arbor, Mich., 1985).

Galsworthy, John (1867–1933), was in his mid-twenties and trained for the legal profession when he first met Conrad, then seaman, in the *Torrens* in 1893. He and his fellow Harrovian E.L. Sanderson had been to Australia and the Far East in quest of Stevenson: they missed Stevenson, but found Conrad. From that meeting developed two of the longest and most equable friendships of Conrad's life. As the senior man and the first into print, Conrad played an important part in getting Galsworthy's fiction noticed when he began writing under the pseudonym of 'John Sinjohn'. He also read many of Galsworthy's early manuscripts and advised, probed and debated with a writer fundamentally different from himself. The faithful and decent Galsworthy reciprocated with constant friendship and support, financial help, hospitality at his London homes, and even proof-reading for his friend. In 1904 Conrad dedicated *Nostromo* to Galsworthy, wrote a review of the latter's *The Island Pharisees* and a preface to Ada Galsworthy's translation of Maupassant. By 1906 Galsworthy had made the transition from amateur to professional writer and found his own direction with *The Forsyte Saga*. Though he went on to gain a public recognition that was denied to Conrad (he was awarded the Nobel Prize for Literature in 1932), his star began to wane from the 1930s onwards.

Garnett, Edward (1868–1937), critic, dramatist, publisher's reader and nurturer of literary talent, was a key influence in the making of Conrad's early career after their first meeting in 1894 (when, as a reader for T. Fisher Unwin's, he recommended *Almayer's Folly* for publication). From then until about 1900 the priceless Garnett was alway at hand as sympathetic friend and mentor, 'creative' reader of Conrad's early manuscripts and regular reviewer of his fiction. In addition, Edward also provided the isolated Conrad with access to the English Edwardian in a much wider sense – notably, to a cultural and social elite with some bohemian fringes and to inestimable professional contacts. Little wonder that Conrad chose to dedicate *The Nigger of the 'Narcissus'*, an important landmark in his career, to Garnett. Though they grew apart in later life, possibly because of Garnett's keen Russophilism, Conrad always acknowledged the value of his early contact with the age's most complete bookman: 'Straight from the sea into your arms, as it were. How much you have done to pull me together intellectually only the Gods that brought us together know. . . . I am proud after all these years to have understood you intellectually' (to EG, Aug 1923). George Jefferson's *Edward Garnett: A Life in Literature* (1982) gives a detailed picture of Garnett's abilities as discoverer of talent and book-surgeon; it also contains chapters on Garnett's home at the Cearne as a literary centre and on the

Mont Blanc literary circle which he founded (and with which Conrad maintained an intermittent connection). Garnett's father, Richard Garnett (1835–1906), was Keeper of Printed Books at the British Museum. Edward's wife, Constance (1862–1946), was a noted translator of Russian writers, especially Turgenev and Dostoevsky, whose translations Conrad read from the late 1890s onwards. Their son David (1892–1981) became a novelist linked with the Bloomsbury group and recalled the Garnett–Conrad era in *Memoirs: The Golden Echo* (1953) and *Great Friends: Portraits of Seventeen Writers* (1979).

Gibbon, Reginald Perceval (1879–1926), or 'Uncle Reggie' as he was affectionately known to the young Conrads, was educated in Germany and worked as a merchant seaman in British, French and American ships before becoming a journalist and man of letters. From 1907 onwards Gibbon, his wife (Maisie) and two daughters were good personal friends of the Conrads, both families spending several holidays together. The relationship between the two men was particularly close during the writing of *Under Western Eyes* and its aftermath (1908–11), when Gibbon provided much moral and practical support. In 1914 Conrad dedicated *Victory* to the Gibbons. During the war Gibbon travelled widely as a journalist and correspondent, keeping the Conrads in touch with Borys's movements at the front. In later years he resided in Jersey, where he died and where Conrad's presumably many letters to him were destroyed in a bombing raid.

Gide, André Paul Guillaume (1869–1951), distinguished French writer of the inter-war years and Nobel Prize laureate in 1947, was introduced to Conrad by Agnes Tobin in July 1911. Already an admirer of Conrad's work and *Lord Jim* in particular, Gide promoted Conrad in the *Nouvelle revue française* circle, supervised a translation of Conrad's works into French, and translated *Typhoon* himself. Though the two met rarely, they continued to read each other's works and corresponded from 1911 until Conrad's death. Gide later dedicated *Voyage au Congo* (1927) to Conrad's memory. See also Frederick R. Karl, 'Conrad and Gide: A Relationship and a Correspondence', *Comparative Literature*, XXIX (1977) 148–71.

Gosse, Edmund (1849–1928; knighted 1925), literary historian, biographer, and author of the semi-autobiographical *Father and Son*

(1907), enjoyed considerable influence in the Edwardian literary establishment. He played a minor and indirect part in shaping Conrad's career, being one of the first readers of the *Almayer's Folly* manuscript and later organising a Royal Literary Fund award for Conrad. Conrad's name was among 200 signatures on a greetings message sent to Gosse on his seventieth birthday.

Graham, Robert Bontine Cunninghame (1852–1936), traveller, writer, pioneer socialist and Scottish nationalist, enjoyed a period of ranching and adventuring in South America before succeeding to the family estate in 1883. As a Liberal MP (1886–92), the colourful 'Don Roberto' was a charismatic public figure, imprisoned after 'Bloody Sunday' in Trafalgar Square (1887), a devotee of William Morris, and often affectionately caricatured – as in Shaw's *Arms and the Man* (1894). The larger-than-life Graham was instantly attractive to Conrad when they first met in 1897 and began a lifelong friendship. Their correspondence between 1897 and 1903 – discussing each other's work, contemporary political events, the history of imperialism, and their own differences of outlook – prompted some of Conrad's richest and most revealing letters. It shows two secure friends testing to the limit their own and each other's opinions, arguing from opposing philosophic corners, but also being surprised into recognising fundamental similarities between themselves – according to Cedric Watts, recognising that each was a blend of Don Quixote and Hamlet. These letters, as well as Graham's own South American writings, were part of the rich matrix out of which Conrad's *Nostromo* grew. For further details on the engrossing relationship between a product of the Polish *szlachta* and a son of the Scottish landed aristocracy (who died in Buenos Aires), see Cedric Watts's introduction in his edition of their letters, and Cedric Watts and Laurence Davies, *Cunninghame Graham: A Critical Biography* (Cambridge, 1979).

Hallowes, Lilian Mary (1870–1950), Conrad's secretary and typist, was virtually a part of the household from 1904 to 1924. She 'used to declare that proofs would be found imprinted on her heart when she died' (*JCC*, p. 228).

Hastings, Basil Macdonald (1881–1928), a minor essayist and dramatist, approached Conrad in 1916 with a plan to dramatise

Victory. During the next three years until the play was performed in 1919, Conrad oversaw the project, enjoyed being involved in its casting, and thought of collaborating on an original play with Hastings. The latter served in the Royal Flying Corps during the war and edited one of its journals, *The Fledgling*, in which Conrad's essay 'Flight' appeared in 1917.

Heinemann, William (1863–1920), founded his publishing firm in 1890 and by the turn of the century had compiled a remarkable fiction list which included Stevenson, Kipling, and Conrad's *The Nigger of the 'Narcissus'*. From 1895 to 1897 Heinemann also published the *New Review* under the editorship of W.E. Henley. In 1921 the Heinemann firm co-published with Doubleday the first collected edition of Conrad's works.

Henley, William Ernest (1849–1903), poet and critic, was also an influential editor and patron whose decision to publish the serial version of *The Nigger of the 'Narcissus'* in *New Review* (1897) marked an important breakthrough in Conrad's early career. Surprisingly the two men seem never to have met, though Conrad corresponded with Henley on the subject of his collaboration with Ford and associated himself with the Henley memorial in 1904.

Hope, George Fountaine Weare (1854–1930), a lifelong non-literary friend from Conrad's early London days of 1880, was an ex-seaman and had sailed in the *Duke of Sutherland* three years before Conrad. As a director of several companies and owner of a leisure craft, the *Nellie* (in which Conrad enjoyed outings in 1891), Hope appears to be remembered in the frame-story of 'Heart of Darkness'. After their honeymoon in 1896, the Conrads settled in Stanford-le-Hope as close neighbours of the Hopes, the two men continuing their tradition of regular boat-trips. Though the Conrads moved from Stanford in 1898, they never lost contact with the Hopes, to whom *Lord Jim* was dedicated.

Hudson, William Henry (1841–1922), born in Argentina, came to England in 1869 and wrote a number of South American romances, and essays on rural England. After first meeting in 1899, he and Conrad met periodically – mainly in the Garnett and Mont Blanc circles – and perhaps shared a feeling of being at the periphery of the literary establishment. Conrad read and reread Hudson's work, remaining a permanent admirer of his style. He wrote a review of *Green Mansions* (1904) in the year of its publication and later commented on the man and his work that 'there was nothing more *real* in letters – nothing less tainted with the conventions of art' (to EG, 22 Aug 1922).

James, Henry (1843–1916), was at the height of his reputation as a novelist when Conrad sent him an inscribed copy of his second novel, *An Outcast of the Islands*, in 1896. James later reciprocated with a copy of *The Spoils of Poynton*, and the two writers met at the Reform Club in February 1897. The exaggerated formality of their early correspondence (much of it in French, with James addressed as 'Cher maître') seems to have extended into the personal relation between two men, who, though close neighbours, were uneasily aware of inhibiting social and cultural differences between themselves. Their personal contact and mutual regard reached its height at the turn of the century, when Ford moved to Winchelsea and, in turn, brought Conrad closer to Lamb House. In 1902 James supported the move to secure a Royal Literary Fund award for Conrad, who soon wrote his respectful 'Henry James: An Appreciation' (1904). Later the two writers modified their opinions of each other's work: Conrad entertained serious doubts about James's last novels (whose falling-off he attributed to the practice of dictation), while James's reservations about *Chance* surface in his *Times Literary Supplement* article 'The Younger Generation' (1914), later reprinted as 'The New Novel' in *Notes on Novelists* (1914). For a comparative view of the two writers, see Elsa Nettels, *James and Conrad* (Athens, Ga., 1977).

Jean-Aubry, G. (1882–1950), adopted name of Jean Aubry, French man of letters and music critic to whom *The Rover* is dedicated, was probably introduced to Conrad by Retinger during the First World War. With Curle, he became an ardent admirer and a regular part of the Conrad circle. After the novelist's death he championed Conrad's reputation in France, becoming a prolific (if not particularly subtle) translator, critic and editor of his work. Conrad's first biographer in the two-volume *Life and Letters* (1927), he also wrote *Joseph Conrad au Congo* (1925; translated 1926) and *The Sea Dreamer: A Definitive Biography of Joseph Conrad* (1957).

Jones, Robert (1857–1933; knighted 1917), specialist in orthopaedic surgery, became Jessie's surgeon and a close friend of the Conrad family from 1917 onwards.

Kliszczewski, Joseph Spiridion (1849?–1932), was the son of an émigré Pole who left Poland after the 1830 insurrection and worked as a watchmaker in Cardiff. On his first visit to the family in May 1885, Conrad became friendly with Joseph Spiridion, wrote him letters which offer the first extant example of his written English, and later took Jessie to spend their first Christmas as a married couple in Cardiff.

Korzeniowski, Apollo (1820–69) and **Ewa**, *née* **Bobrowska** (1832–65), Conrad's parents, were married on 8 May 1856 after a lengthy courtship and in the face of strong opposition from the Bobrowskis, who regarded Apollo as improvident and quixotic. Though both Apollo and Ewa belonged to the *szlachta* or land-owning gentry, their families did not share the same political outlook: the intensely ardent and patriotic Korzeniowskis had been involved in two insurrections against the Russians and had their estates confiscated, while the Bobrowskis, though patriotic, espoused more conciliatory politics. Born in the Ukraine and educated at St Petersburg University, Apollo was at the time of his marriage already becoming known as a translator of English and French classics and as author of two satiric plays, *Comedy* (1855) and *For the Love of Money* (1859). His subsequent writings – ranging from bitter anti-Russian polemic to the poetry of Romantic and messianic commitment – increasingly became the vehicle for a spontaneous overflow of powerful patriotism and linked with the cause of an insurgent Poland throwing off the yoke of her oppressors. Apollo's move to Warsaw in 1861, where he helped to establish the underground Committee of the Movement, marks the culmination of his revolutionary activities. Later that year he was arrested, imprisoned in the Warsaw Citadel and, with his wife, was sentenced to exile. With their four-year-old son, they were escorted to Vologda, 300 miles north-east of Moscow, and later transferred to Chernikhov, near Kiev. Always fragile in health, Ewa died of tuberculosis in April 1865, leaving father and son in lonely exile. In early 1868 Apollo and his son were permitted to move to Lwów (then under Austrian rule) and later to Cracow, where Apollo died in May 1869. His funeral became a large patriotic demonstration, with the 11-year-old Conrad walking at the head of the procession. For contrasting views of Apollo at various stages of his life, the opposition between 'Korzeniowski' and 'Bobrowski' values and their effect on Conrad, see the introduction and contents of *CUFE*, Keith Carabine's review of that volume in *Conradiana*, XVIII (1986) 48–59, and Czeslaw Milosz, 'Apollo N. Korzeniowski: Joseph Conrad's Father', *Mosaic*, VI (1973) 121–40. *CUFE* also contains letters from Ewa to Apollo, as well as the latter's christening poem to his son and his polemic 'Poland and Muscovy'.

Krieger, Adolf Philip (1850?–1918), an American of German origin, first met Conrad when they were fellow lodgers at Dynevor Rd, Stoke Newington, in early 1880, the starting point of a staunch 15-year friendship. As an agent for Barr, Moering and Co. in the late 1880s, Krieger found temporary work for Conrad in the company's warehouse and put him in touch with prospective employers; he also acted as intermediary for the allowance paid by Bobrowski to his nephew and lent Conrad a substantial amount of his own money. These unpaid debts left Conrad under financial obligation to Krieger for several years and appear to have caused their estrangement in 1897. The dedication to him of *Tales of Unrest* 'for the sake of old days' was probably intended to placate Krieger, who – Norman Sherry suggests – may have provided a model for Verloc in *The Secret Agent*.

Lucas, Edward Verrall (1868–1937), essayist, anthologist and biographer of Lamb, was introduced to Conrad by Garnett in 1895. He acted as advisory reader at Methuen for many years, becoming chairman in 1925.

Marris, Carl Murell (1870–?), a sea-captain in the Eastern archipelago and married to a Malay princess in Penang. His visit to Conrad in September 1909 reactivated memories of the East and prompted Conrad's return to Eastern material in *'Twixt Land and Sea – Tales*, which is dedicated to Marris.

Marwood, Arthur Pierson (1868–1916), younger son of a Yorkshire baronet, emerged from Clifton and Trinity College, Cambridge, as a talented mathematician. Poor in health, he was never fit for a career and lived the quiet life of a gentleman farmer in

Kent. Through Ford, who revered him as a living embodiment
of the enlightened Tory gentry, he met Conrad in 1906 and was
later involved with the *English Review* before quarrelling with
Ford in 1909. According to Ford, Marwood was 'a man of
infinite benevolence, comprehensions and knowledges' (*It Was
the Nightingale*, 1934, p. 214). During the period 1908–16 he was,
perhaps, Conrad's closest friend, the 'real Wise Man of the Age'
(to Marwood, 30 Apr 1915) with whom the novelist could regularly
discuss his work and sound out his ideas. With his unliterary
approach to literary problems, Marwood was a refreshing asset
to Conrad and Ford. He also provided a model for Ford's Tietjens
in *Parade's End* (1924–8).

McClure, Samuel Sidney (1857–1949), American publisher, had
founded a newspaper syndicate and *McClure's Magazine* before
establishing his first publishing company in 1897. With various
partners, he published several Conrad titles in America at the
turn of the century. Conrad had many dealings with his brother
and London agent, Robert McClure.

Meldrum, David Storrar (1864–1940), a literary adviser at Blackwood's London Office, was sympathetically and professionally
involved in Conrad's early career (1897–1902) when he oversaw
the publication of 'Karain', the *Youth* volume and *Lord Jim*. The
patient and long-suffering Meldrum mediated between Conrad
and William Blackwood, and valued Conrad's opinion of his
own literary efforts in *The Conquest of Charlotte* (1902). He became
a partner in the firm in 1903 before retiring in 1910.

Morrell, Lady Ottoline Violet Anne (1873–1938), half-sister of
the sixth Duke of Portland, was the patroness of a celebrated
literary and artistic circle at Garsington Manor in Oxfordshire
and later in London. With an introduction from James, she
first visited Conrad's Kent home in August 1913 and later
arranged a meeting between Conrad and Bertrand Russell. For
her impressions, see *Ottoline: The Early Memoirs of Lady Ottoline
Morrell* (1963).

Newbolt, Henry John (1862–1938; knighted 1915), former barrister,
later became a naval historian and patriotic poet. He served as one
of the trustees appointed to administer the Royal Bounty Fund

grant awarded to Conrad in 1905, an episode remembered in his *My World as in my Time* (1932).

Noble, Edward (1957–1941), was an ex-seaman friend of Conrad's with literary ambitions. Conrad passed on his manuscripts to Garnett in 1895. Noble's first work, *Shadows from the Thames*, was published in 1900.

Northcliffe, first Viscount, born **Alfred Charles William Harms-worth** (1865–1922), newspaper proprietor, revolutionised popular journalism in founding the *Daily Mail* (1896) and the *Daily Mirror* (1903). In 1908 he added *The Times* to his vast empire. Conrad's friendship with 'the Napoleon of Fleet Street' developed during the First World War when they both enjoyed the company of Jane Anderson. Conrad wrote articles for the *Daily Mail* and was the object of Northcliffe's patronage and largesse.

Pawling, Sydney Southgate (1862–1922), partner of Heinemann, joined the firm in 1893 and four years later negotiated with Conrad to publish *The Nigger of the 'Narcissus'* and *The Rescue*. A lifelong friend and admirer, and trusty Pawling could be relied on for professional advice. He oversaw the publication of the Heinemann Collected Edition of Conrad's works in 1921.

Penfield, Frederic Courtland (1855–1922), the American ambassador in Vienna during the First World War, was responsible for handling the diplomatic interests of Britain, France, Japan and Italy in Austria–Hungary. Acting as intermediary for the Conrads during their 1914 Poland visit, he helped to secure funds and release permits for them. Conrad gratefully dedicated *The Rescue* to him.

Pinker, James Brand (1863–1922), seems to have begun his working life as a clerk in Tilbury Docks before entering the world of journalism through the *Levant Herald* (in Constantinople) and then (in London) through *Black and White* and *Pearson's Magazine*. In 1896 he started his Arundel Street literary agency and by 1901 acted for Wells, Crane, James, Ford and Conrad. Though much maligned by authors of the day, Pinker served the interests of several 'difficult' writers with a skilful blend of shrewdness, tact, generosity and long-suffering. These qualities were certainly needed in the early stages of his 20-year association with Conrad, who in 1901 was regarded by Pinker (and regarded himself) as an uncertain professional risk. In a relationship where the volatile Conrad required Pinker to play many parts – friend, generous banker, father-figure, general factotum – tension and mutual exasperation were unavoidable. After subsidising the needy Conrad for several years, Pinker's patience snapped in 1909 at a time when Conrad owed him £2700 and was labouring to finish *Under Western Eyes*. A subsequent violent quarrel led to a two-year estrangement. From 1911 onwards, their relationship slowly weathered into genuine friendship: the two men met weekly in London, shared family holidays, and even collaborated on a screenplay. After Pinker's sudden death in 1922, which affected Conrad deeply, his literary agency was taken over by his two sons, Eric and Ralph. For a survey of the 1300 extant letters from Conrad to Pinker, see Frederick R. Karl in *Joseph Conrad: A Commemoration*, ed. Norman Sherry (1976).

Poradowska, Marguerite, *née* **Gachet** (1848–1937), was the wife of Conrad's distant cousin Aleksander Poradowski (1836–90), who had escaped into exile from Poland after the 1863 insurrection and eventually arrived in Belgium, where he met and married Marguerite. Born of French parents in Brussels and by marriage an Austrian subject, the handsome and cultivated Marguerite was a published author by the late 1880s, with a secure place in the literary circles of Brussels and Paris (where she often lived in Passy). Conrad first made contact with the Poradowskis on his way to Poland in 1890, at a time when Aleksander was close to death. For the next five years the friendship between Conrad and the woman and *confidante* whom he addressed as his 'aunt' embraced several meetings and a lengthy correspondence in French, which, on Conrad's part, combines a number of strands – the artistic, distantly romantic, and melancholic. How far their relationship had developed by 1895 or whether Conrad proposed marriage to Marguerite in that year, as Baines speculates, remain open questions. Whatever the truth, their relationship was important to Conrad not only practically (Marguerite helped him to secure a job in the Congo in 1890) but in introducing him to the flavour of the literary life and directing his thoughts towards the idea of publication.

Quinn, John (1870–1924), of Irish descent, a wealthy American lawyer and collector, began purchasing manuscripts from Conrad in 1911 when the latter was desperately short of money. Though they never met, the two corresponded at length, and Conrad continued to sell him manuscripts until 1918, when he found another willing buyer in T.J. Wise. On his 1923 trip to America, Conrad appears to have avoided meeting Quinn. Later that year the sale of Quinn's collection of Conradiana took place at a New York auction and yielded enormous profits for the collector. See also B.L. Reid, *The Man from New York: John Quinn and his Friends* (New York, 1968).

Retinger, Józef Hieronim (1888–1960), a Polish literary scholar active in Parisian literary and political circles, first met Conrad soon after the autumn of 1912, when he arrived in London to enlist support for the cause of Poland's independence and proceeded to supervise a Polish Bureau in Arundel Street. The cosmopolitan Retinger and his attractive wife Otolia accompanied the Conrads on a holiday to Poland in the summer of 1914, a visit that coincided with the outbreak of the First World War. Retinger helped awaken Conrad's feeling for the political fate of wartime Poland, persuaded him to help internationalise the Polish problem, and worked very closely with him on 'A Note on the Polish Problem' (1916), prepared for the Foreign Office. Conrad's essay 'The Crime of Partition', written in 1918, also owes a debt to Retinger, in this case to the latter's *La Pologne et L'équilibre européen* (Paris, 1916). Towards the end of the war Retinger was expelled from Allied countries as a result of social and political intrigues. He went to live and work in Mexico before returning later to the European political arena. In 1941 he published the evocative but often wayward memoir, *Conrad and his Contemporaries: Souvenirs*. See also John Pomian, *Joseph Retinger: Memoirs of an Eminence Grise* (1972).

Reynolds Stephen (1881–1919), a promising young Edwardian prose writer and author of *A Poor Man's House* (1908) and *Alongshore* (1910), met Conrad and Ford through Garnett in 1907. Briefly connected with the *English Review*, he also became one of the circle of young admirers gathered around Conrad between 1907 and 1912, and wrote 'Joseph Conrad and Sea Fiction' (*Quarterly Review*,

1912). See also J.D. Osborne, 'Conrad and Stephen Reynolds', *Conradiana*, XIII (1981) 59–64.

Rothenstein, William (1872–1945; knighted 1931), painter, etcher and lithographer, was born in Bradford (Yorks) and studied art at the Slade School (London) and then in Paris, where he made contact with Whistler, Degas and Pissarro. From about 1898 he specialised in portraits of the celebrated, including Conrad, who first sat for him in 1903. Their friendship developed through Rothenstein's efforts to find subsidies and organise loans for the needy Conrad during his *Nostromo* period. Subsequently Conrad made contact with other artists in the Rothenstein circle and regularly attended the artist's exhibitions. Rothenstein's *Men and Memories* (3 vols, 1931–9) provides a vivid account of their long friendship.

Russell, Bertrand Arthur William, third Earl (1872–1970), British philosopher, mathematician and Nobel Prize laureate in 1950, first met Conrad in 1913 through Lady Ottoline Morrell. At that time undergoing a personal crisis, Russell responded with particular intensity to the 'wonderful' Conrad and the spell of his 'inward pain and terror' (Russell to Lady Ottoline Morrell, 10 Sep 1913). Russell's retrospective (and probably over-coloured) view of a friendship that lasted for a year and then lapsed until 1921 can be found in his *Portraits from Memory and Other Essays* (1956) and *Autobiography, 1872–1914* (1967). An additional reason for their closeness in 1913–14 was that the philosopher wanted the writer's opinion of his earliest attempt in creative writing, *The Perplexities of Paul Forstice* (published in 1972). See Owen Knowles, 'Conrad and Bertrand Russell: New Light on their Relationship', *The Conradian*, 13 (1988) 192–202.

Sanderson, Edward Lancelot (1867–1939), was Galsworthy's travelling companion in 1893 when the two met Conrad in the *Torrens* (see Galsworthy, above). Conrad soon visited 'Ted' in Elstree, where he was about to teach in the family's preparatory school. On subsequent visits to Elstree, Conrad found abundant hospitality, boisterous company with the large family, female friendship, and a cultivated haven where he could bring *Almayer's Folly* to birth, encouraged by Ted and his mother Katherine. *An Outcast of the Islands* was dedicated to Sanderson and *The Mirror of the Sea* to his mother. After serving in the Boer War, Sanderson remained in Africa until 1910, mainly in Nairobi, where he was Town Clerk. On his return to England he became headmaster at Elstree and remained in close touch with Conrad.

Symons, Arthur William (1865–1945), poet and critic, was a leading figure in the British aesthetic movement of the 1890s, when he contributed to the *Yellow Book*, edited the *Savoy* (1896), and wrote the influential *The Symbolist Movement in Poetry* (1899). Conrad and Symons began to correspond in 1908, when the latter sent the draft of an essay on Conrad to the author. As near-neighbours in Kent, the two later met regularly, with Conrad helping to console the depressive Symons, though John Conrad remembered that 'my father rather tended to keep him [Symons] "at arm's length" and never became a close friend' (*Joseph Conrad: Times Remembered*, p. 60). Symons' *Notes on Joseph Conrad* appeared in 1925.

Thomas, (Philip) Edward (1878–1917), devoted two decades to journalism, critical writings and hackwork – in which connection he made an early contact with Conrad in 1910 – before turning to poetry with the encouragement of Robert Frost. A neighbour in Kent, Thomas's intimacy with Conrad developed during the war, but was cut short by his death in the Battle of Arras.

Tittle, Walter Ernest (1883–1966), an American artist, made several sketches and portraits of Conrad after their first meeting in 1922 and helped persuade Conrad to make his 1923 American trip. In 1948 Tittle presented his best-known oil-painting of Conrad to the National Portrait Gallery.

Tobin, Agnes (1864–1939), minor American poetess and translator of Petrarch, enjoyed meeting famous writers and numbered among her friends Alice Meynell, Symons, Yeats, Pound, Gide and – from 1911 onwards – Conrad, who dedicated *Under Western Eyes* to her.

Unwin, Thomas Fisher (1848–1935), founder of the T. Fisher Unwin publishing house in 1882, published Conrad's first novel, *Almayer's Folly*, and two other early volumes. After a difference with 'the Patron' about terms in 1896, Conrad took steps to find an alternative publisher (Heinemann) for *The Nigger of the 'Narcissus'*. Unwin re-established relations with Conrad in his late career, bringing out *The Arrow of Gold* (1919) and *The Rover* (1923).

Walpole, Hugh Seymour (1884–1941; knighted 1937), was born in New Zealand and educated in England, where he worked as a schoolmaster before becoming a freelance writer in 1909. A prolific novelist, he soon won popular literary success, mixed in the best literary circles, and enjoyed the friendship of James, Bennett, Wells and Priestley. Though Walpole wrote a book on Conrad in 1916, the two did not meet until 1918, just after Walpole had returned from Russia. From that date he was a favourite among the many younger writers who regularly gathered round the senior writer at his Kent homes. Conrad read and admired Walpole's two Russian novels, *The Dark Forest* (1916) and *The Secret City* (1919), and wrote a preface to *A Hugh Walpole Anthology* (1921).

Wedgwood, Ralph Lewis (1874–1956; knighted 1924), railway administrator, brother of Lord Wedgwood the politician, met Conrad in 1913 through Curle. In July 1914, Conrad stayed with Wedgwood and his wife in their Harrogate home while finishing *Victory*; he acknowledged their hospitality in the dedication to *Within the Tides*. Wedgwood also acted as one of the co-executors of Conrad's will.

Wells, Herbert George (1866–1946), and Conrad first made contact in 1896, when Wells, then a rising novelist, favourably reviewed *An Outcast of the Islands* in the *Saturday Review*. Conrad was flattered by the notice but bristled privately at some of Wells's criticisms. From the beginning, therefore, their relationship was uneasy and contained the seeds of potential conflict. 1898–1904 represents the high point of their relationship, when, as near-neighbours, they were in close geographical and imaginative proximity. While Conrad admired Wells's scientific romances and delighted in *The Invisible Man* (1895), Wells reciprocated with much practical help and support. Gradually, however, their social and political differences became more marked and Conrad's criticism of Wells's utopianism more explicit. At a meeting with Walpole in 1918, Conrad defined his philosophic quarrel with Wells: 'The difference between us, Wells, is fundamental. You don't care for humanity but think they are to be improved. I love humanity but know they are not!' (Hart-Davis, *Hugh Walpole*, p. 168). Martin Ray has suggested that Conrad's *The Secret Agent*, a novel of 1907 dedicated to Wells, marks their final breach – 'with Conrad paying old debts in the dedication while settling old scores in the text which follows' – 'Conrad, Wells, and *The Secret Agent* . . . ', *Modern Language Review*, LXXXI (1986) 561. Wells responded with thinly disguised caricatures of Conrad in *Tono-Bungay* (1909) and *Boon* (1915), and presents his version of their uneasy relations in *An Experiment in Autobiography* (1934).

Wise, Thomas James (1859–1937), bibliographer and book collector, entered Conrad's sphere in 1918, when he bought from him the first of several manuscripts and paid for the right to publish Conrad's miscellaneous writings in limited-edition pamphlets. He compiled *A Bibliography of the Writings of Joseph Conrad, 1895–1920* (1920). Wise's reputation was irreparably damaged in 1934 by the exposure of his literary forgery.

Zagórska, Aniela, was the wife of Karol Zagórski (died 1898), Conrad's second cousin once removed and Marguerite Poradowska's nephew by marriage. Conrad visited the Zagórskis and their parents in Lublin on his return to Poland in 1890, kept in close touch with the family after Karol's death, and stayed at Aniela's pension in Zakopane in 1914. Her two daughters, Aniela (1881–1943) and Karola (1885–1955), maintained contact with Conrad in his later years, Aniela as one of the first translators of his works into Polish, and Karola as a visitor to Capel House and Oswalds. Their reminiscences are reprinted in *CUFE*.

Locations and Addresses

Aeolian Hall 131–7 New Bond St, London W1.

Arundel St JBP's literary agency was situated here (off the Strand, London WC2) at Talbot House.

Athenaeum Club 107 Pall Mall, London SW1.

Brede Place A large fourteenth-century manor house in Brede (East Sussex), rented by Stephen and Cora Crane in January 1898.

Burys Court JBP's residence at Leigh, near Reigate (Surrey).

Capel House The JCs' home in Orlestone, near Ashford (Kent), from June 1910 to March 1919, Capel House was described by Borys as 'undoubtedly the happiest of the Conrad homes and one in which JC might well have ended his days' had it not been for the fact that the owner 'wanted the house for his own immediate use and gave us six months' notice' – *Joseph Conrad's Homes in Kent*, Joseph Conrad Society Pamphlet (1974) p. 4. Capel House was the family home during the whole of the First World War and saw the beginning of many of the friendships that sustained JC during his later years.

Cearne, The The EGs' country home in Limpsfield (Surrey), also a well-known centre for Edwardian literary figures and intellectuals.

Curzon Hotel Curzon St, Mayfair, London W1.

Gatti's Properly named Gatti's Adelaide Gallery, a fashionable restaurant at Charing Cross, London WC2.

Junior Carlton Club JG's club, situated between Pall Mall and St James's Square, London SW1.

Kettner's Restaurant 37 Greek St, London W1.

Mont Blanc A restaurant in Gerrard St, London W1, in whose upper room a group of writers gathered for regular Tuesday lunch-time meetings. Formed by EG, the circle included Edward Thomas, W.H. Davies, Stephen Reynolds, Hilaire Belloc, Muirhead Bone, FMF and, very occasionally, JC and JG.

National Liberal Club FMF's club, situated at Whitehall Place, London SW1.

Norfolk Hotel 30–2 Surrey St, Strand, London WC2.

Oswalds The last – and largest – of the JCs' homes, which they occupied from October 1919 until the novelist's death, was situated in Bishopsbourne, near Canterbury (Kent). JC liked the house, but not its situation – in a hollow enclosed by woods that did not offer any larger view. It became a place of pilgrimage for the numerous admirers and friends of the ageing novelist and the scene of quite lavish entertaining in JC's closing years.

Pent Farm This old farmhouse in Postling, near Hythe (Kent), was sub-let by FMF to the JCs in October 1898 and remained their home until September 1907. Residence there brought JC nearer to other writers living in the Kent area – notably FMF, Wells, James and Crane – and also allowed him a close proximity to the sea (with Hythe only 3 miles away). At Pent Farm JC also had his first opportunity to play the role of English country squire, though eventually, as Najder observes, he probably developed mixed feelings about the place: 'Jessie later came to regard the years at the Pent as the happiest of her married life. Conrad did not share her view. In his mind the Pent must have been associated with incessant grind and mounting debts. But it was at Pent Farm that Conrad wrote the books ['Youth' to *The Secret Agent*] that establish his greatness and determine his position' (*Joseph Conrad: A Chronicle*, p. 289). For further details, see Borys Conrad, *Joseph Conrad's Homes in Kent*, and Najder, pp. 288–90.

Restaurant d'Italie 52 Old Compton St, London W1.

Romano's A restaurant noted for its fashionable 'bohemian' atmosphere at 339 Strand, London WC2.

Royal Automobile Club 89–91 Pall Mall, London SW1, JC's regular club in the early 1920s.

Sandgate H.G. Wells lived in this Kentish coastal town (near Folkestone) from August 1898, first in lodgings and then at Spade Hall.

Someries The JCs lived in this Bedfordshire house from October 1907 until March 1909. Just before moving in, the novelist described its situation: 'It is in Bedfordshire 40 minutes from St Pancras. . . . It is $2^1/_2$ miles from Luton: a farmhouse of a rather cosy sort without distinction of any kind, but quite 500 ft above the sea – which is what we both want' (to Harriet Capes, 10 Sep 1907). Despite the advantage of being close to London during the eventful period when FMF was establishing the *English Review*, JC soon came to dislike the 'damned Luton place' (to JBP, 18 Sep 1908).

Spring Grove This furnished seventeenth-century manor in Wye, near Ashford (Kent), was lent to the JCs for a temporary stay between March and September in 1919, before they moved to their last home at Oswalds.

Stanford-le-Hope In this Essex village, seven miles north of Tilbury and close to the Thames Estuary, the newly married JCs had their first two homes. JC was initially attracted to Stanford in late 1896 by the prospect of living near his oldest English friends, G.F.W. Hope and his wife, and of resuming with Hope their long-standing tradition of boat-trips together. After a brief period of residence in a semi-detached villa in Victoria Rd, the JCs made the short move in March 1897 to Ivy Walls, a spacious Elizabethan farmhouse, which they rented until October 1898.

Select Bibliography

The three published volumes of the projected eight-volume edition of *The Collected Letters of Joseph Conrad*, ed. Frederick R. Karl and Laurence Davies (Cambridge, 1983–), are an invaluable source of material and datings up to December 1907 (where vol. III ends). Other main sources are listed below. This chronology also owes an obvious debt to Zdzisław Najder's superlative biography, *Joseph Conrad: A Chronicle* (Cambridge, 1983), whose scope and meticulous accuracy make it an essential reference work. Memoirs, biographies, interviews and diaries consulted are too abundant to be listed individually, though the most important of these are included under their appropriate authors in the 'Who's Who' section. For readers interested in exploring further, a helpful guide to almost 300 less well-known reminiscences can be found in Martin Ray's *Joseph Conrad and his Contemporaries: An Annotated Bibliography of Interviews and Recollections* (Joseph Conrad Society, 1988). My final debt, again too great to be detailed, is to the continuing work of an entire community of Conrad critics as found in two indispensable journals, *Conradiana* (Lubbock, Texas) and *The Conradian: Journal of the Joseph Conrad Society, UK* (London). Unless otherwise stated, the place of publication for all books listed below is London.

Allen, Jerry, *The Sea Years of Joseph Conrad* (New York, 1965).
Baines, Jocelyn, *Joseph Conrad: A Critical Biography* (1960).
Beckson, Karl, *Arthur Symons: A Life* (Oxford, 1987).
Conrad, Borys, *My Father: Joseph Conrad* (1970).
Conrad, Jessie, *Joseph Conrad as I Knew Him* (1926).
——, *Joseph Conrad and his Circle* (1935).
Conrad, John, *Joseph Conrad: Times Remembered* (1981).
Conrad, Joseph, *Joseph Conrad: Letters to William Blackwood and David S. Meldrum*, ed. William Blackburn (Durham, NC, 1958).
——, *Conrad to a Friend: 150 Selected Letters from Joseph Conrad to Richard Curle*, ed. Richard Curle (1928).
——, *Letters from Conrad, 1895 to 1924*, ed. Edward Garnett (1928).
——, *Letters of Joseph Conrad to Marguerite Poradowska, 1890–1920*, ed. John A. Gee and Paul J. Sturm (New Haven, Conn., 1940).
——, *Joseph Conrad: Life and Letters*, 2 vols, ed. G. Jean-Aubry (1927).

——, *Joseph Conrad: lettres françaises*, ed. G. Jean-Aubry (Paris, 1930).

——, *Conrad's Polish Background: Letters to and from Polish Friends*, ed. Zdzisław Najder (Oxford, 1964).

——, *Conrad under Familial Eyes*, ed. Zdzisław Najder (Cambridge, 1983).

——, *Joseph Conrad and Warrington Dawson: The Record of a Friendship*, ed. Dale B.J. Randall (Durham, NC, 1968).

——, *Joseph Conrad's Letters to R.B. Cunninghame Graham*, ed. C.T. Watts (Cambridge, 1969).

Ehrsam, Theodore G., *A Bibliography of Joseph Conrad* (Metuchen, NJ, 1969).

Gindin, James, *John Galsworthy's Life and Art: An Alien's Fortress* (1987).

Gordan, John D., *Joseph Conrad: The Making of a Novelist* (Cambridge, Mass., 1940).

Hart-Davis, Rupert, *Hugh Walpole: A Portrait of a Man, an Epoch, and a Society* (1952).

Karl, Frederick, R., *Joseph Conrad: The Three Lives* (New York, 1979).

Marle, Hans van, ' "Plucked and Passed on Tower Hill": Conrad's Examination Ordeals', *Conradiana*, VIII (1976) 99–109.

Marrot, H.V., *The Life and Letters of John Galsworthy* (1935).

Mizener, Arthur, *The Saddest Story: A Biography of Ford Madox Ford* (New York and Cleveland, 1971).

Page, Norman, *A Conrad Companion* (1986).

Sherry, Norman, *Conrad's Eastern World* (Cambridge, 1966).

——, *Conrad's Western World* (Cambridge, 1971).

Smith, Rosalind Walls, 'Dates of Composition of Conrad's Works', *Conradiana*, XI (1979) 63–87.

Stape, J.H., 'The Chronology of Conrad's 1914 Visit to Poland', *Polish Review*, XXIX (1984) 65–71.

Index

1 People, Places and Organisations

Index 155

Clifford, Hugh 37, 49, 50, 78, 79, 103, 122, 124, 129
Cockerell, Sydney 116, 125
Colchester (Essex) 108, 120
Colefax, Lady 104, 118
Colvin family 92, 95, 103, 115
Colvin, Sydney 53, 60, 69, 77, 84, 85, 87, 88, 98, 102, 104,108, 129–30
Congreve, William 105
Conrad, Borys 31, 35, 36, 41, 47, 48, 50, 56, 60, 61, 62, 64, 66, 67, 68, 70, 81, 82, 88, 92, 93, 96, 97, 99, 103, 104, 105, 106, 107, 108, 114, 115, 118, 120, 121, 122, 123, 124, 125, 130
Conrad, Jessie 17, 19, 20, 21, 22–3, 25, 26, 27, 37, 42, 43, 52, 53, 54, 56, 57, 58, 61, 62, 64, 66, 78, 81, 97, 98, 100, 101, 103, 104, 105, 106, 107, 108, 109, 110, 111, 112, 113, 114, 117, 119, 121, 124, 125, 126, 130
Conrad, John 64, 67, 90, 99, 103, 104, 112, 124, 125, 130
Conrad, Philip 123
Corsica 113, 114–15
Courtney, W. L. 30
Cracow 3, 4, 93, 94
Crane, Cora 34, 39
Crane family 31, 37
Crane, Stephen 29, 30, 32, 35, 38, 40, 130
Crippen, Dr H. H. 79
Curle, Richard 78, 86, 87, 88, 89, 92, 95, 96, 108, 110, 111, 112, 115, 116, 117, 118, 119, 120, 121, 122, 123, 124, 125, 126, 131

Dąbrowski, Marian 91
Daudet, Alphonse 20
Davidson, Jo 98
Davies, W. H. 81, 99
Davray, H.-D. 45, 65
Dawson, A. J. 55, 57, 61, 131
Dawson, Ernest 55, 131
Dawson, Francis Warrington 78, 82, 85, 86, 87, 88, 90, 91, 92, 97, 131

Deal (Kent) 53, 112
Delcommune, Camille 14, 15
Delestang, Jean-Baptiste 5, 6
Dent, Hugh R. 125
Dent, J. M. 87, 106, 109, 111
Derebczynka 1
Doubleday family 121, 122
Doubleday, F. N. 71, 88, 92, 107, 112, 116, 121, 132
Douglas, Norman 58, 60, 79–80, 82, 83, 88, 100, 132
Dover 40, 58
Dummett, Elizabeth 97, 103, 111, 118
Dymchurch (Kent) 81

Edinburgh 100
Effendi Hill 121
Elstree (Herts) 17, 18, 20, 69
English Channel 9, 22
English Stage Society 59, 60, 105
Epstein, Jacob 120, 124, 132
Evans, Sir Francis 33
Everitt, S. A. 113, 115

Falmouth (Cornwall) 9
Fecht, Richard 7
Folkestone (Kent) 100
Ford family (FMFs) 36, 38, 40, 41, 45, 47, 48, 49, 51, 72, 75
Ford, Ford Madox 31, 33, 34, 37, 38, 39, 40, 41, 42, 43, 44, 45, 46, 47, 48, 49, 51, 52, 53, 55, 57, 58, 60, 61, 63, 65, 66, 68, 69, 70, 72, 73, 74, 75, 76, 78, 81, 82, 84, 87, 96, 99, 101, 108, 112, 116, 123, 124, 125, 133
Forster, E. M. 114
France 5, 7
France, Anatole 66
Franco-Canadian Transport Co. 17
Frederic, Harold 31
Fresh Air Art Society 88

Galsworthy, Ada 54
Galsworthy family 47, 61, 64, 65, 68, 69, 75, 110, 115

2 Subject Index

CONRAD'S WORKS

OTHER TOPICS